THE TOP 100 DRIVING TEST QUESTIONS

by
ANDREW CROUCH A.D.I., M.I.A.M.
and
JOHN LEVINE A.D.I.

foulsham
LONDON • NEW YORK • TORONTO • SYDNEY

foulsham

The Publishing House, Bennetts Close,
Cippenham, Berkshire SL1 5AP, England

While every effort has been made to ensure the accuracy of all the information contained within this book, neither the author nor the publisher can be liable for any errors. In particular, since businesses change from time to time, it is vital that each individual should check all relevant details for themselves.

ISBN 0-572-02040-6

Copyright © 1997 A. Crouch & J. Levine

All rights reserved. The Copyright Act prohibits (subject to certain very limited exceptions) the making of copies of any copyright work or of a substantial part of such a work, including the making of copies by photocopying or similar process. Written permission to make a copy or copies must therefore normally be obtained from the publisher in advance. It is advisable also to consult the publisher if in any doubt as to the legality of any copying which is to be undertaken.

Typeset in Great Britain by
Rowland Phototypesetting Limited,
Bury St Edmunds, Suffolk.
Printed by St Edmundsbury Press Limited,
Bury St Edmunds, Suffolk.

CONTENTS

	Introduction	5
1	Planning for a test	7
2	The object of the test	15
3	The test requirements	18
4	Some points of interest	34
5	A typical test route	40
6	The theory test	98
7	The results	120
8	Conclusion	122
9	Notes for after the test	123
	Answers to questions in Chapter 6	128

Colour is represented
in diagrams and Highway
Code symbols as shown in
the boxes below

Red

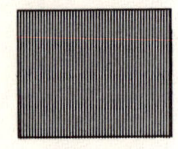

Blue

Diagrams have been adapted from
The Highway Code with the permission
of the Controller of Her Majesty's
Stationery Office.

INTRODUCTION

Driving is a life skill and like any other skill needs a firm grounding and sound practice if it is to be mastered and improved. Current statistics show that less than 50 per cent of candidates pass their driving test in any one year and, with nearly two million people taking the test, that is a staggering one million 'fails' each year. Although the specific reasons people fail are many, the overriding factor is that they are not ready. It is most important to be properly prepared and not to just turn up on the day, hoping for the best.

It is with the aim of providing a firm grounding that this book has been written. It will not make you a driver — only practical experience will do that — but it will give you the knowledge you need to approach your driving test with confidence. We have tried to present the material in as clear and logical a fashion as possible, with preliminary sections on how to plan for your test, what the object of the test is and what will be required of you at the practical test. A typical test route is described, giving concise information as to the points of motoring being tested in each particular situation. Chapter 6 gives details of the theory part of the driving test. Although you will be required to pass this part prior to taking the practical test, typical questions have been given towards the end of the book so that knowledge acquired in the preceding pages can be tested and consolidated. In the final chapters you will find guidance on what happens when you get the test result and points to consider as you start your driving 'career'.

If, by the time you take the driving test, you are able to understand everything in this book and are sure you could handle all the situations mentioned, you will be able to approach your test with knowledge and confidence and we will have achieved our aim.

1
PLANNING FOR A TEST

Q *What form does the driving test take?*
A The driving test is in two parts: the theory test and the practical test, which are organised by different agencies and are completely separate. You must pass the theory test before you can apply for the practical test, which you may take more than once if necessary. The first questions in this chapter relate to the theory test. The remaining questions relate to the practical test.

Q *When should I apply for the theory test?*
A Your driving instructor will advise you when you are ready. You must be 17, have a provisional licence, and know and understand your Highway Code and the other related topics to be covered in the test. For most candidates, a theory test appointment will be available within two weeks of application.

Q *Can I take the theory test at a centre of my choice?*
A Yes, from a choice of 141 test centres.

Q *What form does the theory test take?*
A The theory test is made up of 35 multiple-choice questions, most requiring you to select a single correct answer. Where specified, some may have two or more answers. You will have 40 minutes to complete the test and must gain at least 30 correct answers.

Q *How many people are likely to be taking the theory test at the same time?*
A About 25.

Q *When can the theory test be taken?*
A Theory tests are conducted during weekdays, evenings and on Saturdays.

Q *How do I apply for the theory test?*
A Your driving school will supply you with an application form. Alternatively, you can book by telephone on 0645 000 666 (Welsh-speakers dial 0645 700 201) if paying by credit card.

Q *What if I need more information on the theory test?*
A For more information on the theory test, telephone 0645 000 555.

Q *What do I need to take with me to the tests?*
A Take your signed provisional licence and your appointment card to the theory test centre. For the practical test, take your signed provisional licence, your test appointment card and, if you are taking the test in your own car, your insurance details.

Q *Can I take the theory or practical tests if I am disabled or have other special needs such as learning difficulties?*
A Yes. You must declare any disabilities on the application form and tell the examiner about them prior to the test. The theory test will be available in different languages, and help can be provided for people with reading or learning difficulties.

Q *How do I apply for a practical driving test?*
A Your driving school will supply you with an application form for the test with details of where to apply by post or telephone and credit card.

Q *Can I take the practical test at a centre of my choice?*
A Yes. Your driving school will supply a list of test centres.

Q *What are the age limits for taking the test in a motor-car?*
A You must be at least 17 but there is no upper age limit.

Q *Can I take the test in an automatic car?*
A Yes, but this means that on passing the test you can drive an automatic car only.

Q *Are tests conducted at night or at weekends?*
A Practical tests are conducted from Monday to Friday during office hours, although some test centres offer Saturday tests.

Q *Can I use my own car for the test?*
A Yes, provided everything is legal and in proper working order, and the seat-belts are clean.

Q *Does it help to know the test area?*
A It helps to have a general idea but it is not strictly necessary. Do not confine yourself just to the test area but prior to taking the test, ensure you have had enough practice on all types of road.

Q *Do I need to understand the workings of the car?*
A This is not necessary but you should be familiar with the interior layout of the car, e.g. where the hazard warning lights and the horn are situated. There will be questions in the theory test to ensure that you know how to keep your vehicle in good condition.

Q *How long does the test last?*
A You will be expected to drive for approximately 30 minutes. Generally speaking, from start to finish, about 35 minutes will be spent in the vehicle.

Q *How early should I arrive at the test centre?*
A Allow enough time to find a suitable parking place and to prepare yourself. Rushing prior to the test will only hinder your performance.

Q *How should I dress?*
A You must feel comfortable. The examiner will not be influenced in any way by your style of dress.

Q *Are there toilets at every test centre?*
A No, but there will be some nearby.

Q *Is there a quota of passes?*
A No. You will pass or fail on your own ability.

Q *Can I choose my examiner?*
A No. The tests are allocated on a random basis.

Q *Are there any female examiners?*
A Yes, there are.

Q *Do I have to study the whole of the Highway Code?*
A Yes, and make sure you understand it. Do not learn it 'parrot fashion'.

Q *Will I be asked questions which are not included in the Highway Code?*
A Yes. In the theory test you will be expected to answer questions on all aspects of motoring.

Q *Can someone sit in the back of the car during the test?*
A Yes, with the examiner's permission. If you have difficulty with the language, it may help to have an interpreter. Some candidates like to have their own driving instructor in the car, but remember, he must take no part in the test. Note that on some tests, a supervising examiner may be present but he will have no influence on the result. If you want your driving instructor to sit in, you must obtain the examiner's consent.

Q *Do examiners always follow the same route?*
A No. There are lots of routes and these are varied from test to test.

Q *What books should I read to help me pass the test?*
A When you receive your provisional driving licence, you will also receive a copy of the Highway Code and a leaflet entitled *Your Driving Test*. Both these booklets must be read thoroughly. There are numerous books to help your driving. One of these is published by the Department of Transport and is entitled *Driving*. Other books you will find useful are *Getting it Right: Highway Code Test* by Brenda Ralph Lewis and *Driving Theory Test Quiz* by John Levine, both published by W. Foulsham.

Q *Should I take professional driving lessons?*
A Yes. This is essential because a driving instructor will be trained to make observations on your driving which a friend or relative would probably miss. Many people *do* pass the test without professional lessons, but the observations and remarks made by a qualified instructor will help you avoid many pitfalls in future years.

Q *What happens if I cannot take either test on the appointed day?*
A You are required to give 10 clear working days' notice. If in any doubt read the appointment card carefully.

Q *How do I know if I am ready for the test?*
A When you and your instructor feel you are driving safely and competently at all times, then you are ready.

Q *Should I take a test for experience?*
A You would be better advised to gain more experience before taking the test. Provided you have had enough practice, there is no reason why you should not pass at the first attempt.

Q *Can I drive in bare feet?*
A Yes, if you find it more comfortable, but it is not advisable.

Q *How do I know if my instructor is competent?*
A The best method is to ask a friend to recommend one. Failing this, ensure the instructor you choose displays a badge on the windscreen to show he is fully qualified. All approved instructors must pass rigorous tests before they are allowed to teach. If, for some reason, you are not happy with your instructor, change to another one.

Q *How many lessons should I have had before my test?*
A This is a perennial question with no specific answer. It is impossible for anyone to say until you have had some driving experience. As with any skill, some will master it more quickly than others.

Q *Should I practise in my own car?*
A Yes, if you have one. However, driving experience in *any* suitable car is beneficial and once you have reached a reasonable standard, extra practice helps to build confidence.

Q *Can I remove the head rests?*
A The head 'rests' are in fact head 'restraints' and they are there for a purpose. If, for any reason, you have to stop suddenly they will prevent your head being thrown back and protect you from suffering 'whiplash'. Do not under any circumstances remove them. They are positioned in such a way that they should not interfere with your driving.

Q *What happens if my test is cancelled by the test centre?*
A You will be given another date as soon as one is available.

Q *What do I do when I arrive at the test centre?*
A For the theory test, go into the waiting area where your licence will be checked before you are shown into the test room. For the practical test, park in a sensible, safe place and go into the waiting area where you will be met by your examiner.

2
THE OBJECT OF THE TEST

Anybody who wishes to drive a car, motorbike or any mechanically propelled vehicle is required by law to take a theory test, conducted by DriveSafe on behalf of the Driving Standards Agency (DSA) and a practical driving test before they may drive on any road without restriction. The former regulation was introduced in 1996, the latter in 1936. The theory test was introduced to help new drivers acquire broader knowledge to cope with driving on today's busy roads, which requires greater awareness, responsibility, concentration, patience and attention to detail than ever before. Full details of the requirements are given in Chapter 6.

The object of the practical test is to ensure that you have reached a reasonably high standard to enable you to drive on any road without supervision. You will need to satisfy the examiner that you are a competent and safe driver and that you show courtesy and consideration to all other road users. S/he must be sure you will be able to handle the vehicle you drive in the many and varied situations you are likely to meet on today's busy roads.

Driving examiners are highly qualified drivers who have had to pass rigorous tests of their own driving skills and their ability to notice faults in others. All examiners are bound by a strict code of conduct. They keep their talking to a minimum and will not chat to you. This is to enable you to concentrate on the job in hand.

During the test you must listen carefully to the examiner's instructions. These will be given clearly and concisely. For example, you will be asked to —
'Move away when ready.'
'Pull in on the left.'
'Take the next road on the right,' and so on.

Do not allow your driving to be affected in any way merely because you are being given directions in a formal manner by a stranger. The examiner's mode of speech is simply to ensure all tests are conducted uniformly. There will be nothing personal in the way s/he speaks to you.

As you drive, the examiner will be marking any faults as and when you make them. You are not expected to drive faultlessly however. Mistakes are divided into three categories —

1. Minor mistakes.
2. Potentially dangerous or serious mistakes.
3. Dangerous mistakes.

Only serious or dangerous mistakes will result in failure.

3
THE TEST REQUIREMENTS

Your knowledge of the Highway Code and your attitude to driving will be examined in the theory test already mentioned, and explained in greater depth in Chapter 6.

The practical driving test requirements consist of 21 separate conditions. You will be expected to fulfil all these conditions competently and safely. If you fail your test, you will be given a sheet of paper on which these 21 conditions are laid out and the examiner will underline those on which you failed. Most of the conditions are straightforward, i.e. you either carry them out properly or you do not. But there are others that are open to interpretation. However, as examiners are looking for a safe and competent drive, it is fairly easy for them to make a decision based on their own driving experience, coupled with the prevailing road and weather conditions. We will take each point in turn and describe what is required of you.

1 Comply with the requirements of the eyesight test
The examiner will want to be sure your eyesight is good enough for you to be driving and to this end will ask you to read a convenient number plate.

You must be able to read a vehicle number plate 79.4 mm. (3.1 in.) high

(a) from a distance of 20.5 metres (about 67 feet)

OR

(b) from 12.3 metres (about 40 feet) if you are operating a pedestrian-controlled vehicle such as a power-assisted Post Office handcart.

(N.B. the above figures are taken from the HSMO publication *Your Driving Test*, 1993).

Neither of these should present a problem but, if you are in any doubt, consult an optician. Should you need glasses or contact lenses, you must wear them at all times when you drive.

2 Take proper precautions before starting the engine
Whenever you start the car you must have the handbrake on and the gear lever in

neutral. This usually happens only at the start of the test. However, should you stall for some reason during the test, you must make the car safe by applying the handbrake and selecting neutral before you start the engine again. If you stall on the test, this is counted only as a minor mistake provided you restart the car as described and drive on calmly and safely.

3 **Make proper use of accelerator/clutch/gears/ footbrake/handbrake/steering**
Accelerator — Always use this pedal smoothly. There should be no unnecessary noise or 'racing', so care must be taken when driving under 'clutch control' and you will want to be well practised in this area before you present yourself of examination.
Clutch — The examiner will expect you to have complete control over this pedal. Avoid 'riding the clutch' or jumping your foot off the clutch when changing gear. Do not allow yourself to 'coast' for any distance during the test.
Gears — You are expected to use whichever gear is appropriate at the time and not to stay in a gear too long or change too early. By the time you take the test, gear changes should be positive and smooth. There should be no fear attached to driving in the higher gears.
Footbrake — The footbrake should be used progressively when needed. If you have to brake harshly this will show you have not

assessed the situation ahead in enough time. Good anticipation is vital to good driving.
Handbrake — You must use the handbrake only when it is needed. It must not be used to slow the car down but only to hold the car when stationary.
Steering — There are many faults that arise from improper steering. Firstly, you must ensure you do not cross your hands or let them drop into your lap. If you do, you could be failed. Secondly, you need to maintain your proper road position at all times. Thirdly, never drive with your hand on the gear lever except when making a gear change.

In all the above points, what is uppermost in the examiner's mind is the smoothness of the drive.

4 Move away safely/under control
Safely — To move away safely you must be sure you will not interfere with any other road user. This necessitates careful observation of the road ahead, the mirrors and the blind spots. Special care must be taken to check for pedestrians or cyclists — your examiner will be watching for this.
Under control — You are required to show the examiner that you can drive smoothly away on any gradient or angle. This will be checked specifically when you are asked to perform a hill start or to move away when

pulled in closely behind a parked car.
Correct use of clutch control will be needed
to ensure a progressive start.

5 **Stop the vehicle in emergency/promptly/under control**
You will generally be tested on this in the
early stages of the test. It must be done
quickly, as you would if a real emergency
arose. The examiner will not expect you to
allow the car to skid. So this manoeuvre
should be practised on both wet and dry
roads prior to the test. (N.B. Pregnant
women will be expected to make an
emergency stop in the normal way.)

6 **Reverse into a limited opening either to the right or left under control/with due regard for other road users**
This manoeuvre is to show the examiner
that you can handle the car in reverse gear.
Most people find this difficult simply
because they have not had enough practice
driving in reverse. You can overcome this by
practising more than most! Although the
examiner will not expect your reverse to be
perfect, s/he will expect it to be reasonably
competent.
Under control — You need to keep the car
reasonably close to the kerb and make
smooth progress. The road you reverse into
could be uphill, downhill or flat, and the
corner could be sharp or slightly curved.

Your practice needs to be on all types of corners.

With due regard for other road users — When you are reversing all other road users will have precedence over you so, should a vehicle approach or a pedestrian wish to cross the road, you will need to wait for them. Keep a lookout, and stop if necessary.

7 **Turn round by means of forward and reverse gears/under control/with due regard for other road users**

The purpose of this exercise is to show the examiner you can manoeuvre your car in a restricted space.

Under control — The examiner will expect you to have complete mastery over the clutch and will want you to judge the size of the road accurately. *Do not hit the kerb.*

With due regard for other road users — As with the reverse, all other road users will have precedence over you. Should a vehicle approach while you are doing this manoeuvre, you must wait and allow it to pass. Should someone signal you to continue, do not simply follow his instruction; take care that the road is clear all around before continuing.

8 **Reverse park, under control, with due regard for other users**

The purpose of this exercise is to show the examiner you can manoeuvre the car in reverse gear into a confined space under control whilst keeping a proper lookout so that you do not interfere with other road users.

9 **Make effective use of mirror(s) well before signalling/changing direction/slowing down or stopping**
The use of mirrors is of paramount importance when driving. Merely looking in the mirror when you remember is not good enough. What an examiner looks for is 'effective use' of the mirrors. It is vitally important that you know what is around and behind you at all times and then act on what you see.
Signalling — You need to check carefully every time well before you signal. The examiner will want to be sure that you take notice of what you see and act accordingly. For example, should you be asked to turn right, do not simply follow the instruction. You must ensure no vehicle is coming up to overtake. If there is, then you may need to wait until it has passed before turning.
Changing direction — If you want to overtake another vehicle, to change to another lane or drive round a bend, you will need to check your mirrors first. The examiner will notice if you do not. The side or wing mirrors should be used in conjunction with your internal mirror when necessary.
Slowing down or stopping — When you are approaching a hazard in the road, e.g. a pedestrian crossing, effective use of the

mirrors will enable you to time your braking to arrive smoothly at the hazard. Do not forget this; it is extremely important to know what is behind you at all times and how close it is.

The use of the mirrors should have been practised and understood at the early stages of learning so that by the time of the test you are proficient and sure that you can assess situations quickly.

10 Give signals where necessary/correctly/in good time
Where necessary — Give signals if it will help or warn any other road user, including pedestrians. In the test situation, if you are in any doubt it is better to signal than not to do so.
Correctly — You must use only those signals found in the Highway Code and must never wave anyone on. After signalling with your indicator, you must check it has cancelled when it is no longer needed. Should the indicator cancel before you have completed your manoeuvre, the examiner will expect you to restart it. Conversely, the signal must be cancelled after you have made the manoeuvre.
In good time — A signal needs to be shown early enough for it to be effective. Let the examiner see that you give other road users time to react to your action.

The use of signals covers hand signals as

well as indicators. You will not be specifically tested on hand signals but you need to know them. The examiners do not want to see excessive use of the indicators but will penalise you if you do not use them when needed. For example, if you indicate unnecessarily to overtake a parked vehicle, and there is a junction to the right you could be wrongly informing other road users that you intend to turn the corner. In that instance, it would constitute a serious mistake.

11 Take prompt and appropriate action on all traffic signs/road markings/traffic lights/signals given by traffic controllers/other road users
There is a great deal of information on the road and you must be able to assimilate this information and react to it, e.g. should you see a national speed limit sign and the road is clear you will be expected to pick your speed up accordingly. The examiner will not warn you of any given situation but will take note of how you react. The examiner is not there to trap you, s/he is there to ensure that you handle situations calmly, reasonably and safely.

Traffic signs — The traffic signs are distinctive in their shape, each shape having a specific meaning. Examples are given later in the book and the examiner will expect you to respond to them.

Road markings — All markings painted on the road have a specific purpose too, and you must obey them. As with the signs, there are examples later in the book.

Traffic lights — You must be aware of the difference between traffic lights and Pelican lights and be able to show the examiner that you can act accordingly with each one.

Traffic controllers — In the rare event of the police or a traffic warden directing the traffic, follow their signals, as they will take precedence over any signs or road markings.

Other road users — Great care must be taken when reacting to the signals of other road users, e.g. if a pedestrian at a crossing waves you through, be careful there are no other pedestrians about who are acting independently of this signal. When following another vehicle, especially a bus, you need to be aware of the driver's use of indicators. It could mean s/he intends to turn a corner or pull in to the side. The examiner will be watching to see that you act positively and safely.

12 **Exercise proper care in the use of speed**
Obviously you must always drive at a speed that you can handle. This will vary under different conditions, e.g. if the roads are wet you will need to leave more room to stop. A busy road will need to be negotiated more slowly than an open road. You must, of course, drive within the speed limits at all times.

13 Make progress by driving at a speed appropriate to the road and traffic conditions/avoiding undue hesitancy

A common misconception with the test is that, if you drive slowly you won't make mistakes. Unfortunately, the very fact that you are driving slowly is a mistake in itself. The examiner will expect you to have reached a degree of competence that will enable you to keep your driving flowing. If you hesitate unnecessarily at a junction when the road is clear, then the examiner may feel that you are not fitting in with the prevailing road and traffic conditions.

14 Act properly at road junctions

Regulate speed correctly on approach — As you approach a junction you should arrive smoothly and safely. The examiner will expect the correct and controlled use of the footbrake and gears.

Take effective observation before emerging — When you arrive at the junction you must be certain the way is clear before you commit yourself to entering the road. If you are in any doubt, pause and check again.

Position the vehicle correctly before turning right — When turning right at a junction, whether entering or exiting a road, you must put the car into a position that will enable you to do it safely and without hindering other traffic. Take special notice of road markings and parked vehicles. For further explanation of what is required, turn to pages 56-8, 78-9 and 93-6.

Position the vehicle correctly before turning left — As with a right turn, care must be taken to note any road markings and parked vehicles that may obstruct you. For further explanation of what is required, see pages 51-3 and 59-60.

Avoid cutting right hand corners — If you have taken the correct position for a right turn you should not cut the corner. However, you risk cutting the corner if you turn the wheels too early. If you are not yet confident about right-hand turns, then give them more practice. Cutting corners is a very dangerous thing to do as you will be in a position where you cannot clearly see any approaching vehicle. A severe view will be taken of this if you do it on your test.

15 Overtake/meet/cross the path of other vehicles safely

Overtake — There may be occasions on the test when it is necessary to overtake a slower vehicle. The examiner will need to be sure you have assessed the situation in plenty of time. Ensure it is safe to do so, check the traffic all round and signal if necessary. The examiner will be watching to see if you cut in on the vehicle you have overtaken so allow enough room before you return to the left. Extra care must be taken when overtaking cyclists, so leave as much room as is possible to be safe and to show

the examiner that you know that this is necessary. If in doubt, do not overtake.
Meet — You could find yourself in a narrow road or a road where parked cars make it impossible for two cars to pass. If another vehicle approaches, you will need to look for a safe place to pull over and allow the other vehicle through. It may be easier for the other driver to give way to you but if you are unsure that she will, slow down and move over yourself at a convenient place. To enable you to do this, you will need to look as far ahead as possible.
Cross — When turning right into a minor road you must give way to oncoming traffic. This will mean you have to time your arrival at the junction, slowing earlier if necessary. Refer to Chapter 5, section 20, for further explanation.

16 Position the vehicle correctly during normal driving

You need to keep an even position on the road throughout the test. You should not hug the kerb or stray into the middle of the road. As a general rule, one metre from the kerb will be correct. You should practise in a variety of roads to feel confident that you can keep an even distance from any obstruction to the left.

17 Allow adequate clearance to stationary vehicles

When passing parked vehicles, at least one

metre must be allowed. Should someone open a door unexpectedly or step out from behind a car, this will leave enough time for both of you to react. If it is not possible to leave one metre you will need to drive slowly and the examiner will want to see that you are prepared for the unexpected.

18 Take appropriate action at pedestrian crossings
Where pedestrians have precedence, at a Zebra, Pelican or controlled crossing, you must stop for them. By assessing the situation in advance you should not have to brake violently to achieve this. Uppermost in the examiner's mind will be the safety of other road users, especially pedestrians, who are very vulnerable.

19 Select a safe position for normal stops
During the test you will be asked to pull in on the left on a number of occasions. Sometimes, you will be told exactly where to pull in and at other times you will be asked to find a convenient place. Try to pull in reasonably soon after you are told but remember that the examiner will expect you to understand that you should not obstruct other road users, i.e. do not park outside a drive, opposite a junction, opposite a car in a narrow road or where it would be illegal to park.

20 Show awareness and anticipation of the actions of pedestrians/cyclists/drivers
Pedestrians — Particular care must be taken

with the very young and the very old. As
you are driving, be on the lookout for the
signs that children may be about, e.g. a
child's bike at the side of the road, a
football and particularly ice-cream vans. If in
doubt, assume there is a pedestrian hidden
from view and be ready to stop if necessary.
Cyclists — The majority of us have been
cyclists at some time or another and have
no doubt cursed the driver who was too
close or 'cut us up'. When driving, always
keep your distance from a cyclist and if it is
unsafe to pass keep back. Assume the
cyclist will weave about and wobble and be
ready to act accordingly. When turning left
into a road a cyclist may be overtaking you
on the inside, that is, the left-hand side.
You will need to keep a check on cyclists
whether in front, at the side or behind
you.
Drivers — Other drivers may not be
concentrating as hard as you and could do
something careless or thoughtless. If you
assume all other drivers may not be
concentrating, you will be ready to react
when they do something silly. Over 90 per
cent of accidents are caused by human
error.

21 Ancillary controls

During the test, you will be expected to
demonstrate your understanding of the use
of ancillary controls on the car. For instance,
if the car windows were misting up, the

examiner would expect you to know how to use the de-misters and use them appropriately.

The examiner will want to be sure that you will treat *all* other road users with the same courtesy and consideration that you would expect yourself.

It is by assessing your ability on these 21 requirements that the examiner will reach a decision. During the test s/he carries a standardised form on which s/he marks any mistakes as you make them. An examiner also has other details to complete on this form, such as the prevailing weather conditions, so if you see that s/he is making notes it does not necessarily mean you have failed. All mistakes you make, including minor mistakes, must be noted but do remember you will only fail on *dangerous* or *serious mistakes*. Try to concentrate on what you are doing and take no notice of what the examiner is writing.

4
SOME POINTS OF INTEREST

Q *Do I open the door for the examiner?*
A No. S/he has some details to take concerning the car, so will get in after you.

Q *Do I check s/he has shut his/her door?*
A You are in full charge of the vehicle, so if you are in any doubt ask him/her to check.

Q *Should I tell him/her to wear his/her seat-belt?*
A No. Driving examiners are exempt from wearing them. Most choose to do so, a few may not.

Q *Do I adjust the mirror when I get into the car?*
A Yes, you should adjust the mirror properly when the examiner is sitting beside you and prior to starting the engine.

Q *If I set my mirror so that I have to move my head to see in it, will this impress the examiner?*
A No. When you look in the mirror you should move only your eyes. The examiners are trained to notice eye movements.

Q *Will I drive on a dual-carriageway?*
A This is possible.

Q *Can I drive faster than 30 m.p.h.?*
A You must follow all road signs so if you enter an unrestricted road, i.e. one where the national speed limit of 70 m.p.h. applies, and the road is clear then you should pick your speed up accordingly.

Q *Will I be asked to drive into a cul-de-sac?*
A You may use a cul-de-sac to reverse or turn the car round so if you are told to drive into one then do so.

Q *Should I always indicate without exception?*
A It is not necessary if no-one is around but keep a lookout for other road users including pedestrians and people sitting in parked cars. You should indicate if it helps another road user.

Q *Can I let the wheel slide back through my hands?*
A No. Provided you are driving safely there will always be enough time to feed the wheel back through your hands.

Q *Can I cross my hands?*
A No. The rim of the wheel should be fed through your hands, and you will be penalised if it is not. The reason is that if you need to cross your hands, the examiner will know that you were taking a corner or a bend faster than you could really manage safely.

Q *Should I stop at every junction?*
A You must always stop at STOP signs. At other junctions, be prepared to stop but, if the way is clear, the examiner will expect you to continue.

Q *What if the car rolls back on a hill?*
A By the time of your test you should have complete mastery over the clutch so the situation should not arise. If in doubt, use your handbrake.

Q *Can I use the gears to slow the car?*
A No, you should use the brakes to slow the car and select the correct gear for the speed. Brakes are adequate to cope with anything but the steepest hill. When you brake, the stop lights show up to warn drivers behind you; braking through gears does not produce this warning to others.

Q *Do I have to use fourth gear?*
A If you are driving along an open road and have reached the right speed then the examiner will expect you to use fourth gear.

Q *Do I have to change gear in strict sequence every time?*
A No. Use whatever gear is necessary for the situation. If you are turning from a main road into a small side road then the examiner will view a move from fourth to second as good driving technique. And if you come up to a STOP sign, to continue straight ahead then third to first is the simple way.

Q *Can I wave someone on?*
A No. You must use only those signals that are in the Highway Code. It can be very dangerous to wave someone on.

Q *If someone flashes their lights at me, do I obey?*
A You must be sure it is safe to proceed — keep a good lookout for other road users. Flashing headlights are merely a 'warning of presence', and should not be acted on automatically.

Q *Should I flash my lights?*
A It is better not to do so.

Q *Can I sound my horn?*
A Yes, if it is necessary to prevent an accident — but do not use it as a rebuke. It should not normally be necessary if you are driving sensibly, however.

Q *Should I acknowledge someone if they let me through?*
A Merely nod or smile but do not take your hands off the wheel.

Q *Can I drive through the painted lines marking a bus stop?*
A Yes.

Q *Can I drive through a bus lane?*
A As you approach it there will be a sign informing you of the times it is closed to ordinary traffic. Make sure you allow yourself enough time to read it, because the examiner will expect you to abide by its instructions.

Q *Must the turn in the road be done in three?*
A No. The examiner will ask you to 'turn the car round by means of forward and reverse gears'. So, if the road is a narrow one, it may take five turns. Whatever it takes, do not hit the kerb.

Q *What happens if I think I am going to touch the kerb on the 'reverse'?*
A Stop immediately. Drive forward, straighten the car up and reverse again. Provided you do this carefully, you will not necessarily be failed.

Q *Can I take my seat-belt off for the 'reverse'?*
A Yes, but remember to put it on when moving away again.

Q *Can I stop on the 'reverse'?*
A Yes, as many times as you need in order to look out for other traffic.

Q *Is the 'reverse' always round a left-hand corner?*
A If you take the test in a van, then you will reverse round a right-hand corner, but for cars a left-hand corner is always used.

Q *What do I do if someone drives down the road into which I am reversing?*
A You must give way to all other road users when you are reversing so you will have to go round and start again.

Q *What if a pedestrian wishes to cross the road behind me when I am reversing?*
A As with other road users you must give way and allow them to cross before continuing with the 'reverse'.

5
A TYPICAL TEST ROUTE

The map (Fig. 1) on the opposite page includes all the elements you are likely to meet on a test. In this chapter, below each section heading, you will find the test requirements. By following the numbers on the map and referring back to Chapter 3, you will be able to see what you need to do and exactly what the examiner is looking for at each point.

1. The examiner will meet you in the waiting room where s/he will call your name and ask you to sign a form. This is to ensure you are the correct person taking the test, by comparing your signature with the one on your application form. You are not usually asked for your appointment card but have it with you should s/he need to check. You will then be asked to lead the way to your car.

Fig. 1

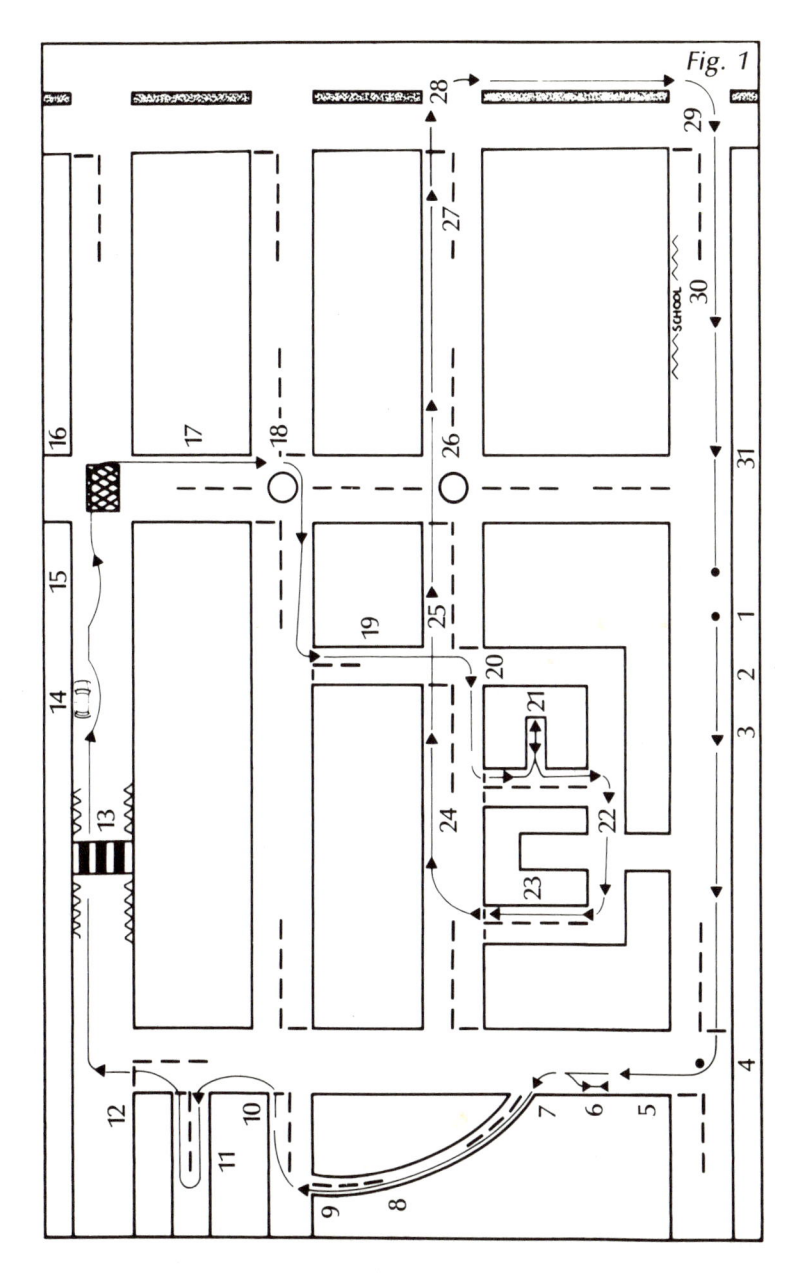

2 Going to the car

Test requirement: 1

On the way to the car you will be asked about any disability that may affect your driving. You will then be asked to read a number plate other than your own. When you arrive at your car the examiner will tell you to get in while s/he takes some details of the car. S/he will be noting the registration number, tax disc and the general condition of the car, including tyres. You should, of course, have satisfied yourself by now that the car is fully roadworthy. While s/he is checking the car, make yourself comfortable, put on your seat-belt and make sure the mirror is properly adjusted. Once in the car s/he will say to you, 'I would like you to follow the road ahead unless I ask you to turn or pull in. Drive on when you are ready please.'

3   The start

Test requirements: 2, 3, 4, 9, 10, 20

The examiner will be looking for a safe start. S/he will be fully aware that you will be nervous and should you make an ungainly start will not mark it against you. However, should you be unsafe, i.e. forget to look over your shoulder, this will constitute a serious mistake. At the early stages of learning to drive you should have formed a sequence, namely — **Mirror, Signal, Manoeuvre** (msm) and this sequence should be an automatic action. The sequence follows a logical pattern —

(a) **Mirror** — including looking around to make sure all is clear.
(b) **Signal** — to inform all around of your intentions.
(c) **Manoeuvre** — taking the necessary action, positively.

You must follow this sequence at all times. It is not good enough to look in your mirror after you have signalled as the look in the mirror is to ensure it is safe to signal. Remember to check your mirror well before indicating.

When pulling away from the side of the road, it is extremely important to check over your shoulder. Also check any places you cannot see in your mirrors. These are known as 'blind spots'.

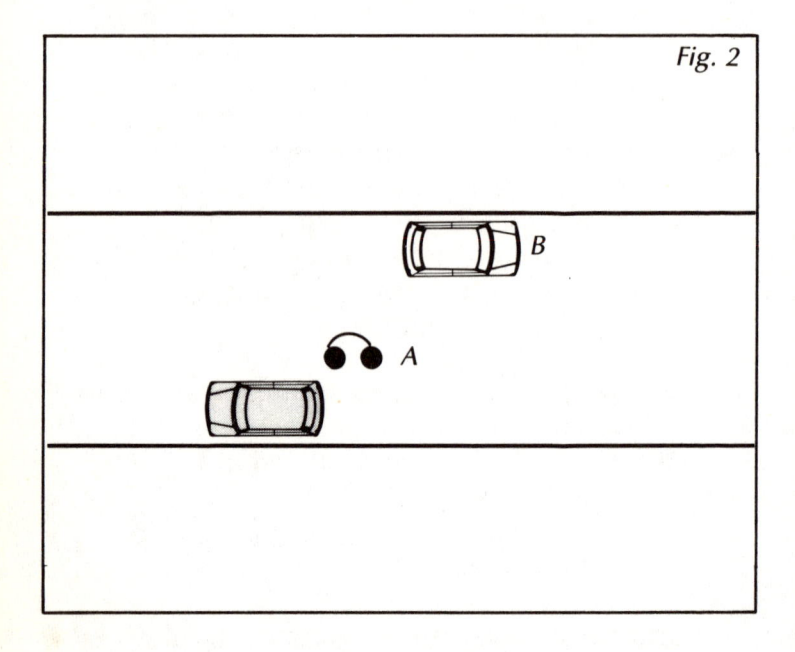

Fig. 2

If there is a cyclist at **A** or a parked car at **B** (Figure 2), you would not be able to see either in your mirrors.

Following the start, the examiner will let you drive for a minute or two to allow you to relax.

4 A mini-roundabout

Test requirements: 3, 9, 10, 14, 15, 20

As you approach the roundabout the examiner will inform you in plenty of time that he wishes you to turn right. Remembering your **M**, **S**, **M** routine, take up a safe position. Approach the roundabout in second gear and, if you are able to see the road to the right is clear, then proceed steadily round. Should a vehicle be approaching from the right, you must give way to it. If the area is small, you may drive over the paint on the road.

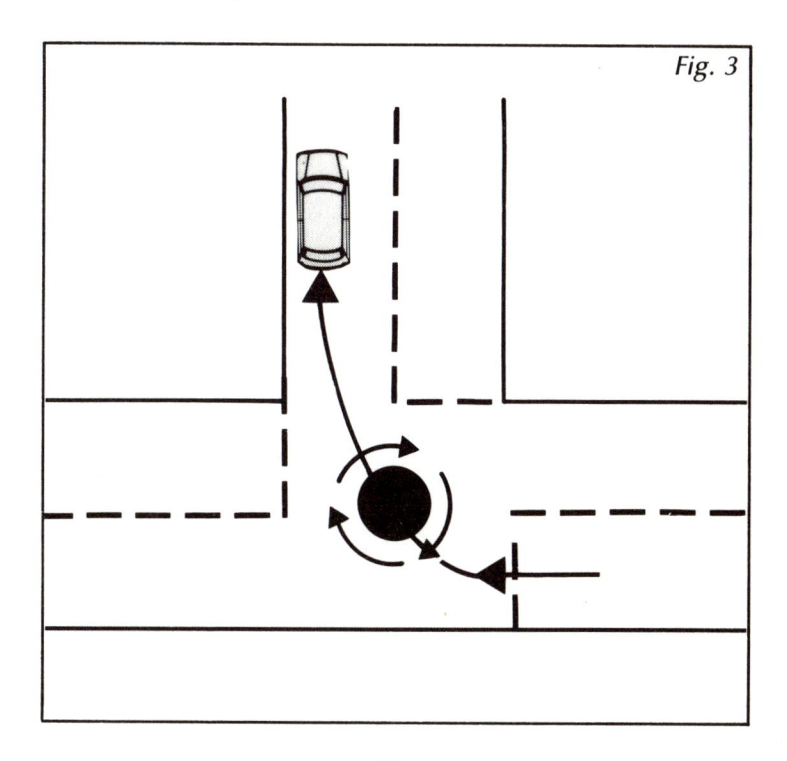

Fig. 3

5 The 'emergency stop'

Test requirements: 4, 5

You will be asked to pull in to the left and the examiner will then inform you of what s/he requires and the signal s/he will give when s/he wants you to stop. As you pull away, build up your speed steadily as you would under ordinary circumstances. When s/he gives you the signal, brake firmly and at the last second, press down the clutch to stop the car stalling.

If you skid, it will be because you have stamped on the brake. Should this happen, release the brake and immediately try again. At all costs keep the car straight on the road. The examiner wants to see a quick but controlled stop; s/he will not be impressed if you slam to a stop and the car slides. This exercise needs to be practised from the early stages of your learning, so you always know how to react if a real emergency should arise. Do not worry about the wear on your brakes; safety must always come before economy when driving. Once you have stopped, put the handbrake on and the gear lever into neutral. You will then be asked to drive away when ready; as you drive on, check for other traffic, looking over both shoulders and in your mirror.

6 Reverse parking, under control, with due regard for other road users

A candidate will be asked to perform two out of the three manoeuvres of Parking in reverse gear, Turning the vehicle round in the road or Reversing into an opening.

If the Examiner wishes to see you park close to the kerb using reverse gear, s/he will ask you to stop on the left behind a parked vehicle. You will then be asked to drive forward and position your car alongside a parked vehicle so that it is possible to reverse back and park close to the kerb within a maximum space of two car lengths. You must 'Park Pretty' and manoeuvring must be kept to a minimum.

This is a 'set' exercise which should be carried out as follows:

1. Stop on the left.
2. Move away (having first carried out the mirror-signal routine and checked over the right shoulder to see if all is clear).
3. Position your vehicle half a car's length beyond vehicle 'B' (see diagram) and not more than 3 feet (1 metre) from the side of vehicle 'B'.
4. After ensuring (by all round observation) that it is perfectly safe to manoeuvre backwards, begin reversing slowly in a straight line, making sure that you are not causing an obstruction to any other road user including pedestrians.

5. When the rear of your vehicle is level with the rear of vehicle 'B' and still moving very slowly, apply slight left lock to bring your vehicle towards the kerb.
6. Still moving very slowly backwards and ensuring that you will not come into contact with point 'X' (see diagram), apply more left lock to bring the back of your car towards the kerb.
7. When you can see that the front of your car is clear of point 'X', begin applying right lock, remembering to make all round observation first.
8. When your vehicle is almost parallel with the kerb, and still moving very slowly, apply left lock to bring all the wheels parallel to the kerb.
9. Try not to move back more than one and a half to two car lengths.
10. When parallel with the kerb you should 'Park Pretty' so that you have enough room to move off safely at an angle from behind the vehicle 'B'.
11. Remember all round observation when the examiner asks you to move on again.

Tips to assist you parking:

1. SLOW SPEED
2. Clutch control.
3. 'All round' observation.
4. Try to complete the manoeuvre by 'parking pretty'.

Parallel parking in reverse gear. **Providing there is a gap of at least one and a half times the length of your vehicle, you can park between two vehicles in reverse gear. When you are clear of vehicle 'B', use your offside door mirror to check when the side of your vehicle lines up with point 'Z' on the vehicle behind you. At that point, begin applying right lock to bring the front of your car towards the kerb.**

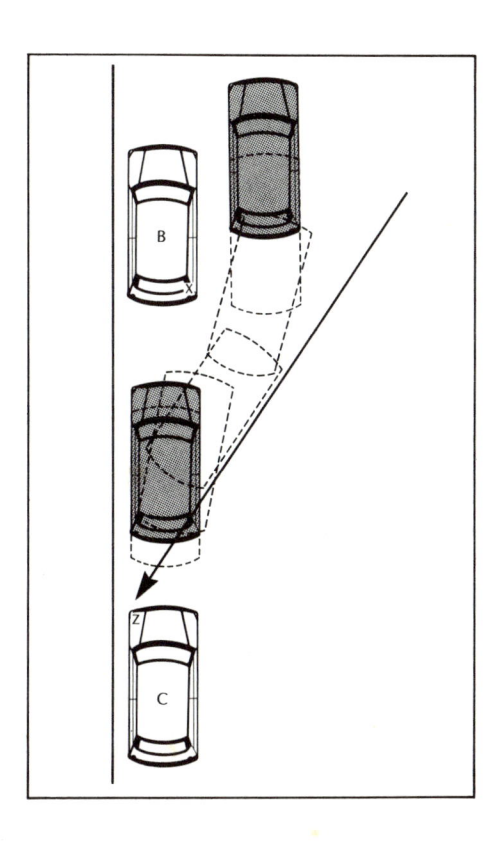

7   Turning left into a road

Test requirements: 3, 9, 10, 14, 20

As you approach the junction, assess the situation. Suppose there is a left turn into a narrow road. Should a car be driving towards you in the road it may be on your side, so you will need to take the corner slowly enough to be able to cope with this. Any pedestrians crossing the road have precedence, so allow them to cross first, stopping if necessary.

A general rule with corners is:
>   *First gear leaving*
>   *Second gear entering*

Following this rule will give you enough time to check for traffic. Do not do otherwise unless the roads and your view of them are obviously clear.

The shape of junctions vary and you will be expected to deal with each junction as it is. Fig. 4 shows three possible situations you may meet.

Fig. 4

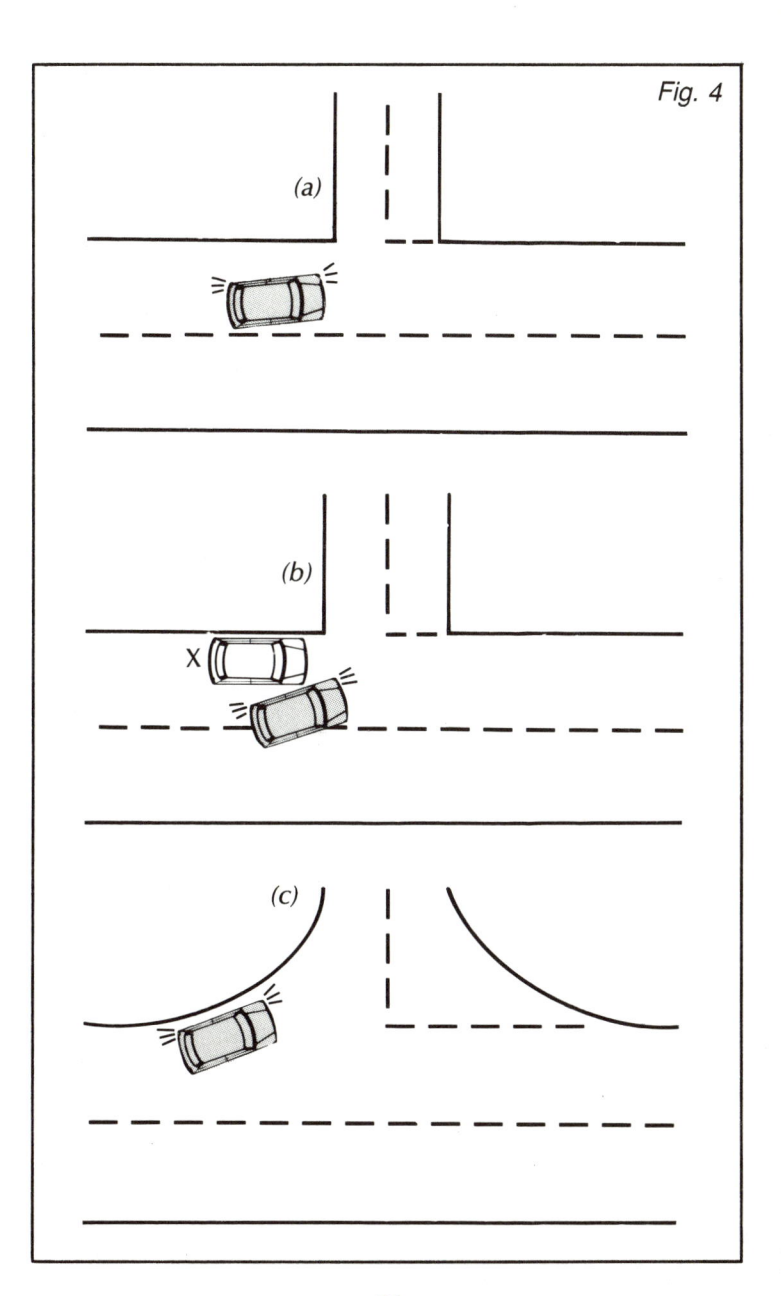

(a) Turning into a narrow road means you need to give yourself more time, so take the corner slowly.

(b) On today's busy roads, a corner where there are no obstructions is the exception rather than the rule. Should a car be parked near the corner at **X** you may need to take the corner more widely to avoid it.

(c) More of a bend than a corner, so your car should follow the bend in the road. If all is clear it may be possible to take a corner like this in third gear.

8 A narrow road with a bend

Test requirements: 9, 12, 15, 17, 20

You will need to check well ahead and, should a car approach from the other direction, find a convenient place to pull in. With the bend in the road, ensure you stay on the left at all times, if possible.

With the car approaching, as in Fig. 5, you have a choice of two places to pull into. If you can slow down in enough time, wait at **A** but do not rush yourself because if necessary you could always move into **B** while the other car waits opposite.

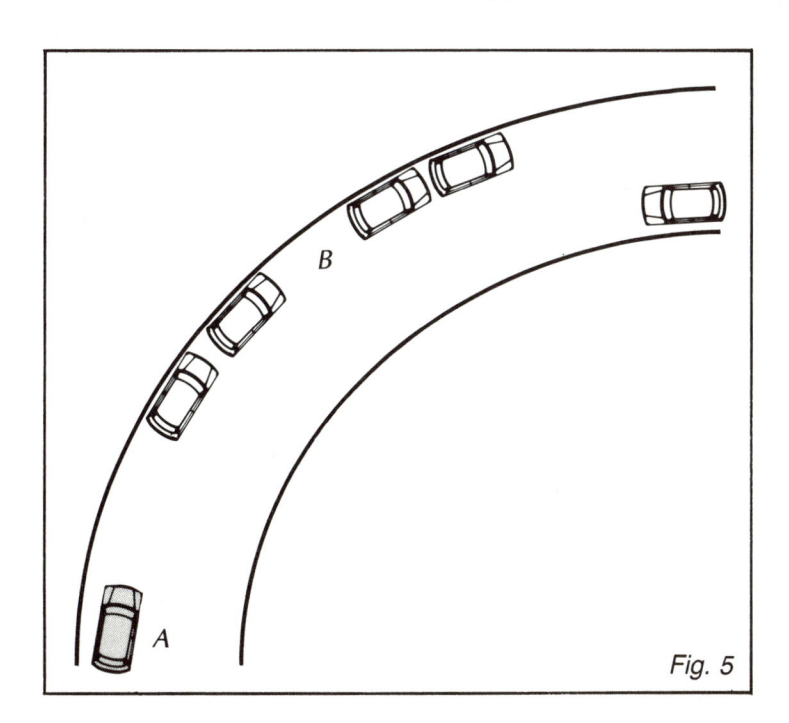

Fig. 5

Fig. 6

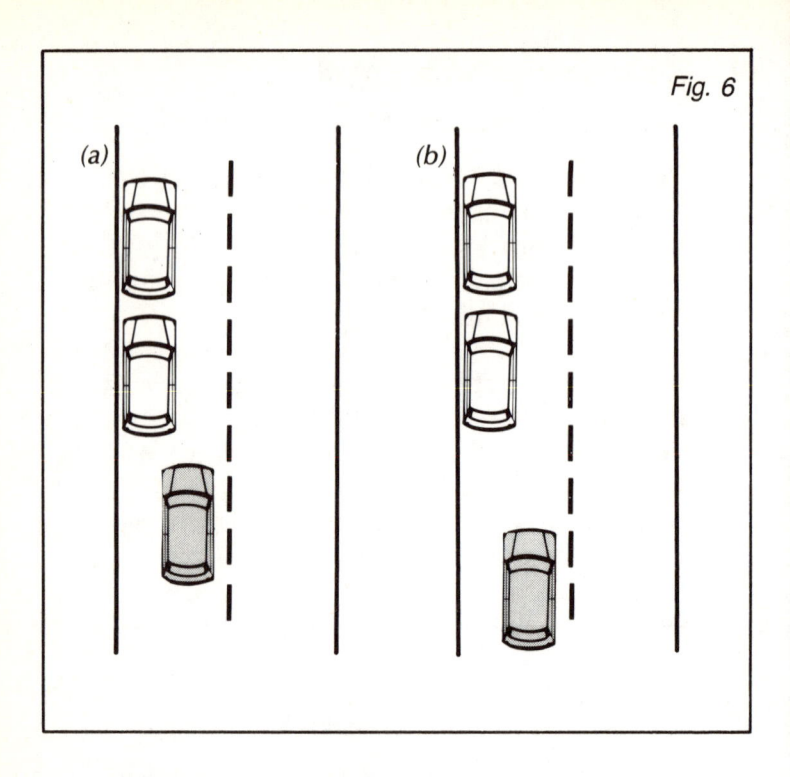

When giving way to a vehicle from the opposite direction, always slow the car down before moving over as this will give you enough time to take up a good position.

In Fig. 6 (**a**), the driver has made it very difficult to drive on by getting too close to the parked car.

In Fig. 6 (**b**), the car is sufficiently out of the way to let an opposing vehicle through but has still left enough room to drive on comfortably.

9 Right turn out (emerging)

Test requirements: 3, 9, 10, 14, 20

As you approach the end of the road, be sure you take up a position well to the left to enable another vehicle to turn into the road. As you need to give way, you will require first gear, but, should the road be clear, you do not need to stop. However, if you are unsure, then do stop and check again.

Fig. 7 shows three possible situations you may meet when making a right-hand turn out.

(**a**) With a narrow road, the car needs to be positioned well to the left.
(**b**) At an ordinary junction you should be just left of the centre of the road. If there are no road markings you must judge where the centre line would be.
(**c**) In this diagram the parked car makes the road narrow and so you will need to keep to the left, leaving enough room for a vehicle turning in.

In all cases, your wheels should be straight at the end of the road and you should start turning them only as you emerge.

Fig. 7

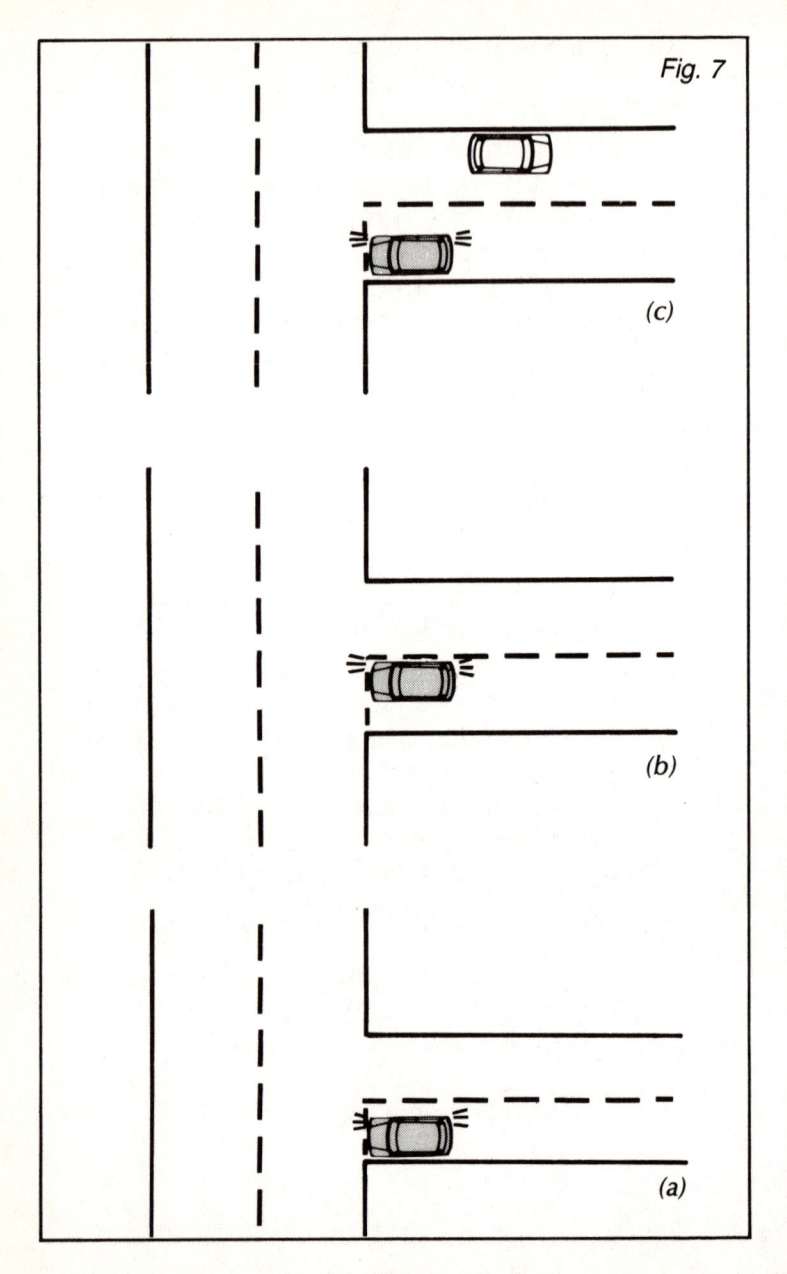

(c)

(b)

(a)

In towns, turning right out of a road is where the majority of accidents happen. If there are parked cars or other obstructions blocking your view, as in Fig. 8, you must creep slowly out to a point where you can see clearly both ways. If a vehicle comes towards you, give way. Some may stop to let you out but others will drive round you.

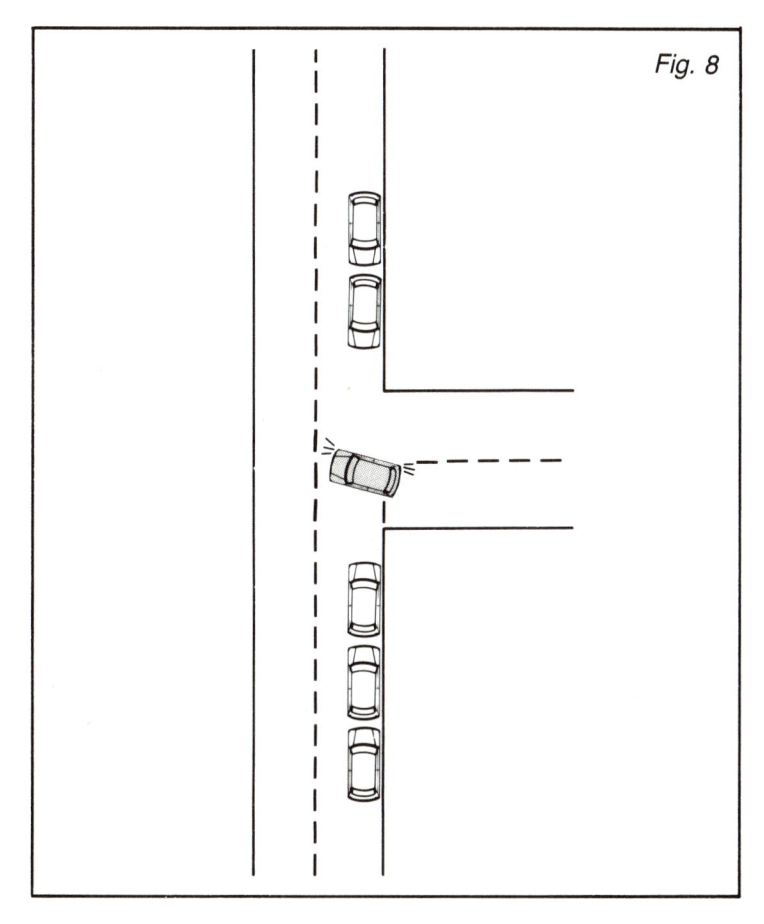

Fig. 8

10 Turning left out of a road (emerging)

Test requirements: 3, 9, 10, 14, 20

As you arrive at the end of the road the examiner will be looking for a smooth and regulated approach (see Fig. 9). If all is clear, you should be able to slip into first gear while looking out for traffic. Provided you have looked right, left and right again and you are sure it is safe to move out without impeding anyone (including pedestrians) then you need not stop. As mentioned earlier, you may be able to drive

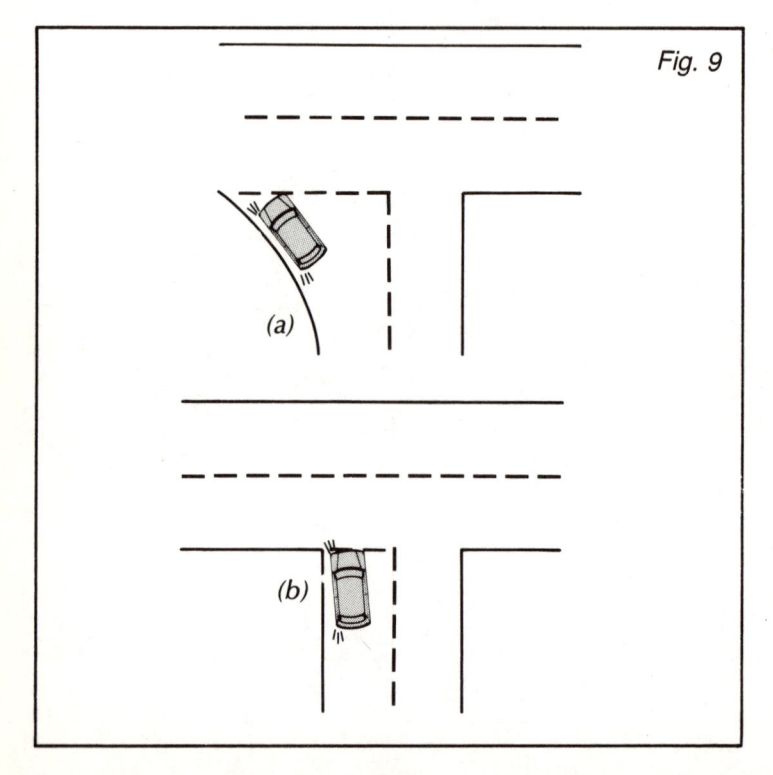

Fig. 9

58

on in second gear but if you are in any doubt, use first. Always keep a careful look out for cyclists.

(a) You will need to tuck into the corner and follow the bend round.
(b) As you arrive at the junction, keep the car about 45 centimetres (18 ins.) from the kerb and turn the wheels, ready to emerge on the left-hand side of the main road.

11 Turning in the road

Test requirement: 7

For the 'turn in the road', you will be asked to pull into the side of the road where the examiner will explain what s/he requires. S/he will say to you: 'Turn the car around by means of forward and reverse gears. Try not to hit the kerb.'

Although it is usually possible to do this exercise in three movements, on a narrow road it may take five. Provided you do not hit the kerb and you keep the car under control at all times, it does not matter how many moves you take. (See Fig. 10.)

(**a**) When you are sure the road is clear, drive slowly to the other side, turning the wheel quickly to the right. About one metre (3 feet) from the kerb, turn the wheel back to the left as much as you can, ready for the next stage.

(**b**) Stop and apply the handbrake, then checking carefully for traffic and being prepared to wait, select reverse gear. Reverse back slowly, turning the wheel quickly to the left. Approximately one metre from the kerb, turn the wheel back to the right, ready to drive on.

(**c**) Stop and apply the handbrake. Check for traffic and select first gear. If all is clear, drive on without touching the kerb.

Fig. 10

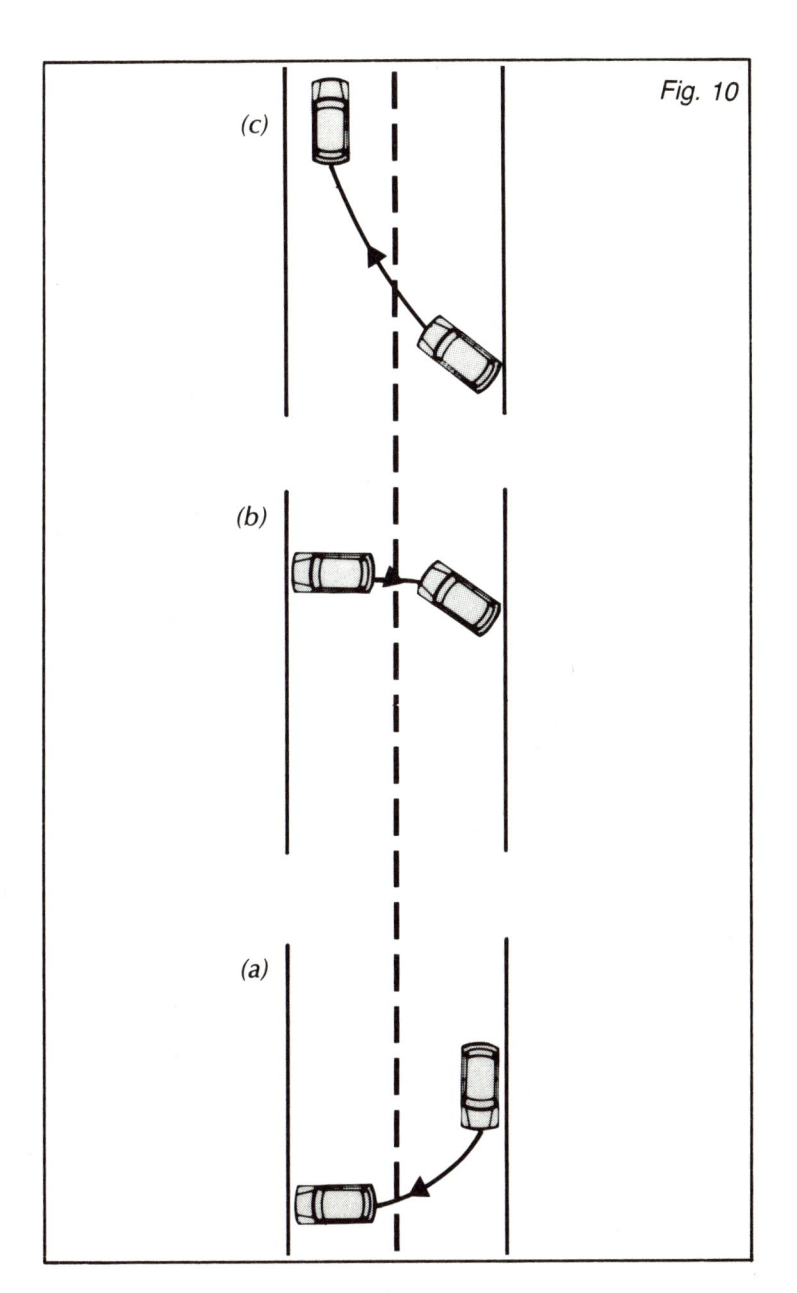

The examiner will not choose a busy road to do the 'turn in the road', but should another vehicle come along, you must allow it to pass. Should a vehicle decide to wait for you, do not allow the driver to put you off; just concentrate on the job in hand. Extra care must be taken with cyclists as they can pass where there isn't enough room for a car. This is one of the few occasions where you may take your seat-belt off, but it is not advisable, as you will continue driving when you have finished and will not pull into the left again.

You do not need to indicate at the start of the 'turn in the road', as you should be doing this manoeuvre only if you are sure the road is completely clear.

This manoeuvre is included in the driving test to show your ability to control the car in a restricted space. The next time you put this exercise into practice could be in a busy car park where the equivalent of the kerbs would be other cars, hence the importance of not hitting the kerbs. The examiner cannot be expected to pass you if you are likely to cause mayhem the next time you go shopping.

12 STOP sign

Test requirements: 3, 9, 10, 11, 13, 20

It is most important that you realise you have arrived at a STOP sign and not an ordinary 'Give Way'. The signs are very distinctive and you will be failed if you do not stop. This should make things easier as you can concentrate solely on your position and not worry whether the road is clear enough for you to continue. Unless the road is on a hill, there is generally no need to use the handbrake.

13 Zebra crossing

Test requirements: 3, 9, 11, 18, 20

The examiner will expect you to notice the crossing well in advance and act accordingly. As you approach, keep a careful look out for any pedestrians near the crossing, taking special care if children are about as they may rush out without looking. At a Zebra crossing, pedestrians have precedence once they put a foot on the actual crossing. However, if they are waiting at the side, you should stop for them, anyway. If a 'helpful' pedestrian waves you on, first take great care to check that there is no-one else around.

14 Moving off at an angle

Test requirements: 3, 4, 9, 10, 17, 20

The examiner will ask you to pull into the left, reasonably close to the car in front, and then to drive on again. This is a situation you will meet many times in your life and the examiner must be sure you are able to perform it safely. S/he will want to see good clutch control and careful observation and signalling. (See Fig. 11.)

(a) This is how the manoeuvre should be performed.
(b) This shows you have tried to do it too fast and have not used the clutch to full effect.

Although you must, obviously, practise this manoeuvre prior to the test, it is wise to leave it until you are happy with your use of the clutch before you use somebody's else's car. Incorrect use of the clutch could be very unfortunate and cause damage.

Fig. 11

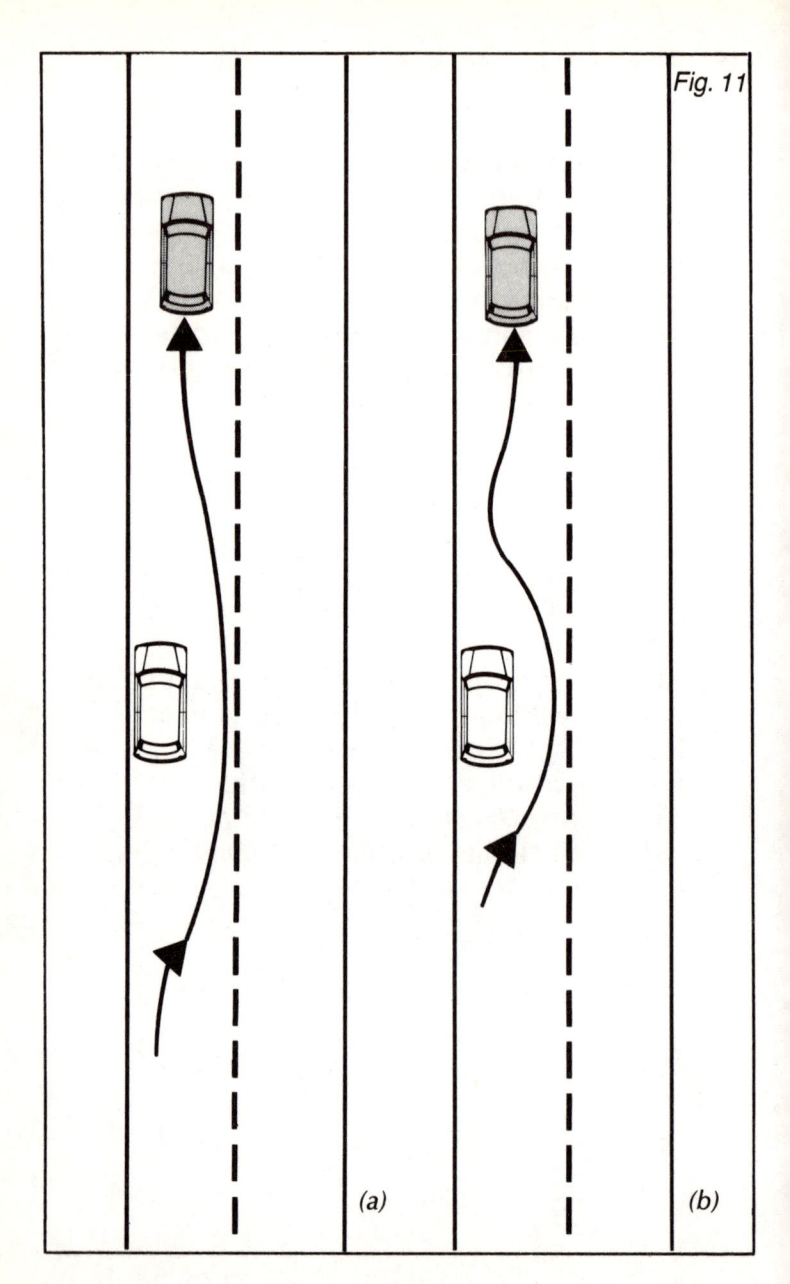

(a) *(b)*

15 Overtaking

Test requirements: 3, 9, 10, 13, 15, 16, 20

Should you find yourself behind a slow vehicle, e.g. a milk float, and it is safe to overtake, you will be expected to do so. Ensure you check all around (using the mirror-signal-manoeuvre sequence) in enough time to be able to move out smoothly. An indicator will warn everybody, including the other driver, that you are overtaking so it should always be used on occasions like this. (See Fig. 12.)

(a) This is how the action should be performed. You should cancel your indicator at **X**.

(b) Here the driver of the vehicle overtaking has come too close and then, when past, has moved back in too early.

Overtaking is always a dangerous manoeuvre, as you have to drive on the other side of the road. In the Highway Code there are lots of occasions where you are told not to overtake. Always check it is safe and legal to do so before you commit yourself and, if you are at all unsure, hang back and wait.

Fig. 12

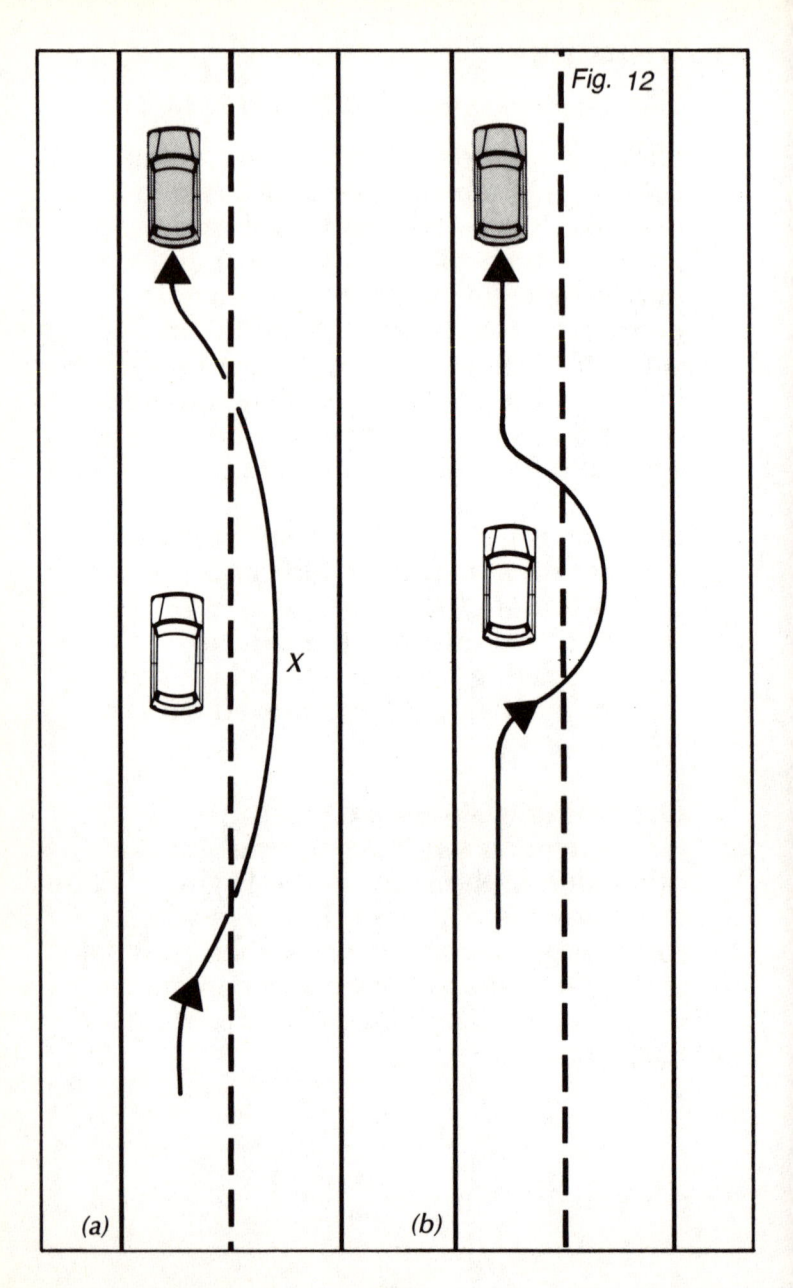

(a) (b)

X

16 Traffic lights with a box junction

Test requirements: 3, 9, 10, 11, 14, 20

Although there will be a lot of information to take in here, provided you know and understand the Highway Code, it should provide no problem.

Take it step by step. If the lights are green and the road to the right is clear (i.e. your exit from the box is not blocked) drive onto the box and wait for oncoming traffic. Should the lights change back to red while you are waiting in the box, you must drive on when it is safe as you would hinder traffic by staying put. If the lights are red or the road to the right is not clear, wait behind the line. (See Fig. 13.)

(a) Wait here if the lights are red or the exit road is blocked.
(b) Wait here if the lights are green but traffic is approaching from the road opposite and your exit from the box is clear.

The rules of a box junction state: 'Do not enter the box unless your exit road is clear.' In Fig. 13, the exit road is marked. As the road is clear, by obeying the rule you may enter the box and wait for oncoming traffic.

Fig. 13

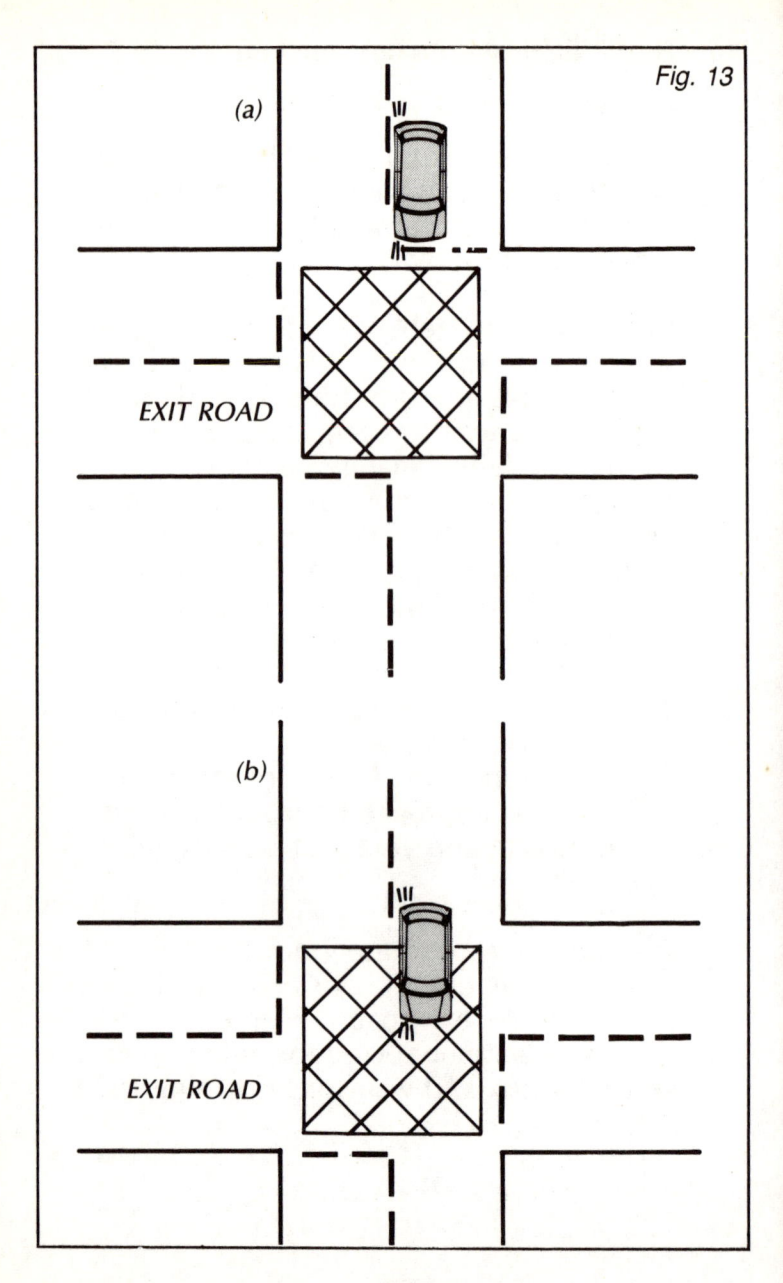

(a)

EXIT ROAD

(b)

EXIT ROAD

Fig. 14

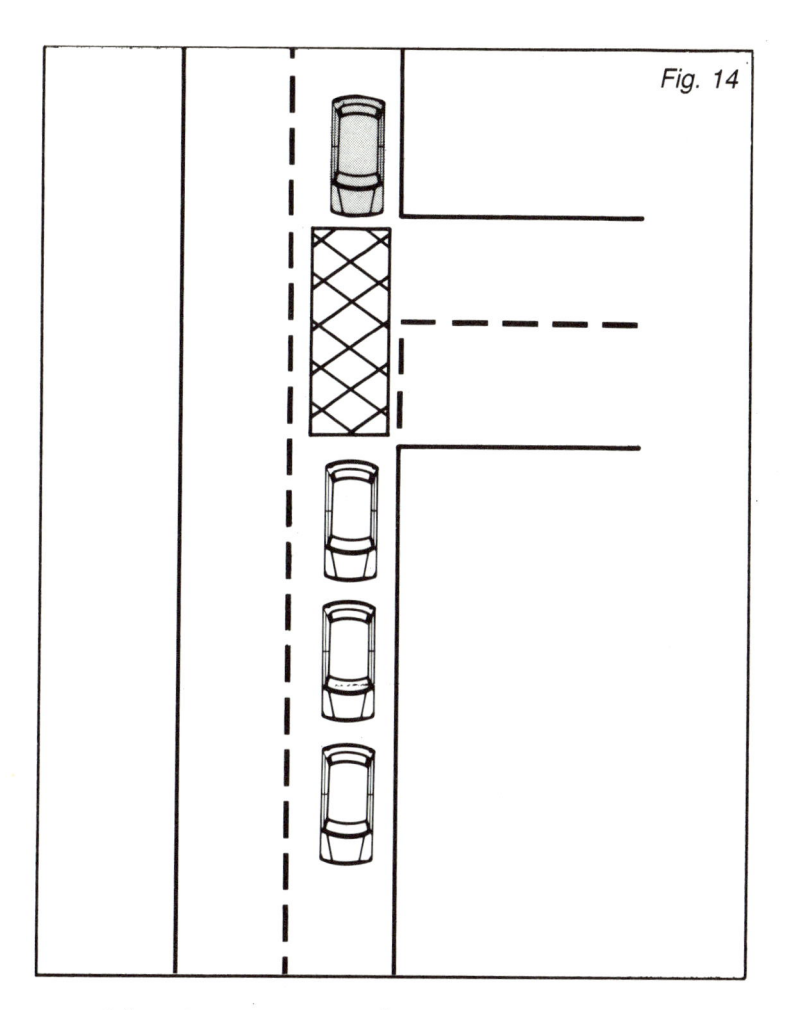

A box junction merely emphasises what should be common sense: to leave a junction clear. If, as in Fig. 14, you cannot clear the junction because there is a car on the other side, you must wait in front of it and allow traffic to enter or leave the side road.

Although we only have one set of traffic lights on our imaginary test, you may well meet more on *your* test, and you will obviously come across them all the time when driving after passing your test.

As you approach traffic lights, you must be prepared for every eventuality. If the lights are green when you first see them, they could change back to red as you get closer — so check your mirror and be prepared to stop. This does not mean you should slow down or change gear unnecessarily. You can stop in any gear if you have to. If the lights change when you are too close to stop in a controlled manner, then drive through the amber light. If you find you have to drive through a red light this will be because you have approached too fast and you will be penalised accordingly.

If the lights are red when you first see them, be prepared for a change to green, if necessary by changing from fourth to second gear.

When waiting at red lights, use the handbrake. Excessive use of clutch control harms the engine and, should your foot slip, it could be very dangerous. You have plenty of time to prepare when the lights change as you must not move until they change to green. Red and amber lights together mean 'stop'.

17 A busy road

Test requirements: 11, 12, 16, 17, 20

In a busy road there will be more things to look out for so your speed will need to be slow enough to enable you to take in all that is happening. There are numerous situations that could arise. A child could run out between parked cars, a driver could pull out without looking, etc. Obviously things such as these could happen anywhere but, where there are more people about, the likelihood of their happpening is greater. Being an experienced driver, the examiner will be aware of what is happening but you, of course, cannot rely on this to help. If the car you are driving is not fitted with dual controls s/he may not be able to do so. In any event, by the time you go for your test you should be able to deal with situations such as these.

18 Right turn at a roundabout

Test requirements: 3, 9, 10, 11, 13, 14, 15, 20

The purpose of a roundabout is to keep traffic flowing, so you will be expected to continue on if the way is clear. The examiner will inform you in plenty of time as to which exit s/he wishes you to take off a roundabout. As you are turning right this time, you will need to move safely over to the centre of the road as you approach. By changing down to second gear, two to three car lengths away from the entrance, you should be allowing yourself enough time to check to the right and, if all is clear, continue.

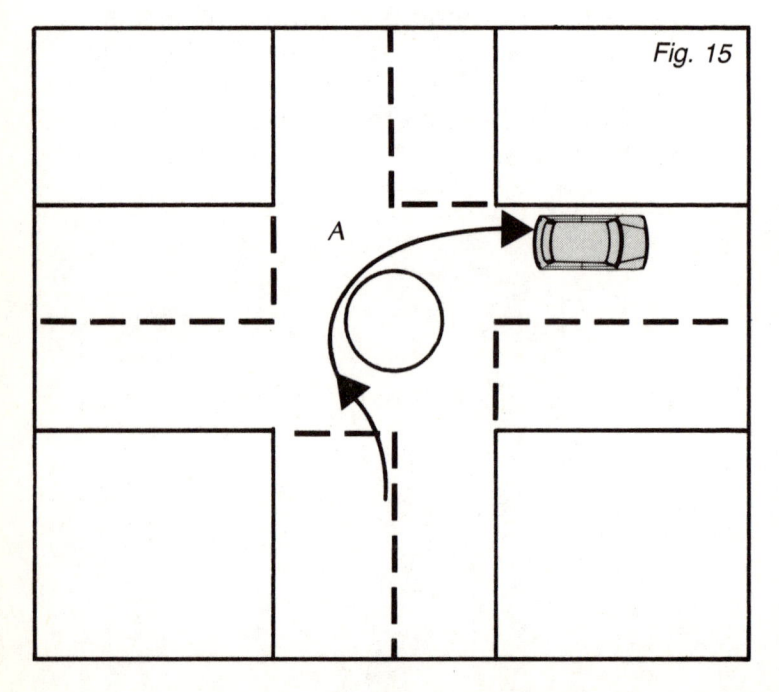

Fig. 15

As seen in Fig. 15, you should stay close to the centre of the roundabout and, as you come off, move to the left.
Indicate right as you drive onto the roundabout and then flick your indicator to the left at **A**, having first checked your mirror.

Although roundabouts vary in shape and number of exits, the rule to follow is straightforward — give way to the right. Before taking your test, you will need to practise on various roundabouts so that even the busy ones hold no fear for you.

19 The 'hill start'

Test requirements: 4, 9, 10, 19

At some stage of your test, you will be asked to pull in on a hill to show the examiner you can drive off on a gradient. It is imperative you do not roll back on this manoeuvre. You should be able to co-ordinate the clutch and accelerator pedals well enough to be able to hold the car stationary when the handbrake is released. Every time you pull out from the side of the road you need careful observation and correct signalling. If you are unhappy with your ability to control the pedals, you may find you jump away and don't leave enough time for checking your blind spots.

The correct order in which to do this exercise is as follows:
(1) Select first gear.
(2) Check the mirror. If it is not clear — wait.
(3) When it is clear, find the biting point and release the handbrake. Hold the car stationary.
(4) Check the mirror again and indicate.
(5) Look over your shoulder and drive away.

If you follow the above procedure, you will not have to hold the car for too long at the biting point and so will not put too much wear and tear on the clutch plates — and your nerves.

20 Turning right into a road (approaching)

Test requirements: 3, 9, 10, 14, 15, 20

When turning right into a side road, you must signal your intentions early enough to warn any vehicles behind not to attempt to overtake. If you have to wait for traffic approaching, take up a position with the front of the car opposite the middle of the road you wish to turn into. If there is no traffic approaching, take care when you turn that no pedestrians are crossing the road into which you are turning. (See Fig. 16.) Do not cut the corner.

(a) If the road is clear enough, this is the position you should take before turning.
(b) If there are parked cars or an obstruction near the corner, ensure you leave enough room for approaching vehicles to drive through.

Approaching a right turn, if traffic allows it, try to time your arrival so that you can continue without stopping. If there is an oncoming vehicle travelling at such a speed that it will arrive at the junction at the same time as you, slow down a little earlier and turn behind it. Do not race to the junction in order to beat it. You will be failed for not 'crossing the path of other vehicles safely'.

Any vehicles turning right out of the side road should give you priority.

Fig. 16

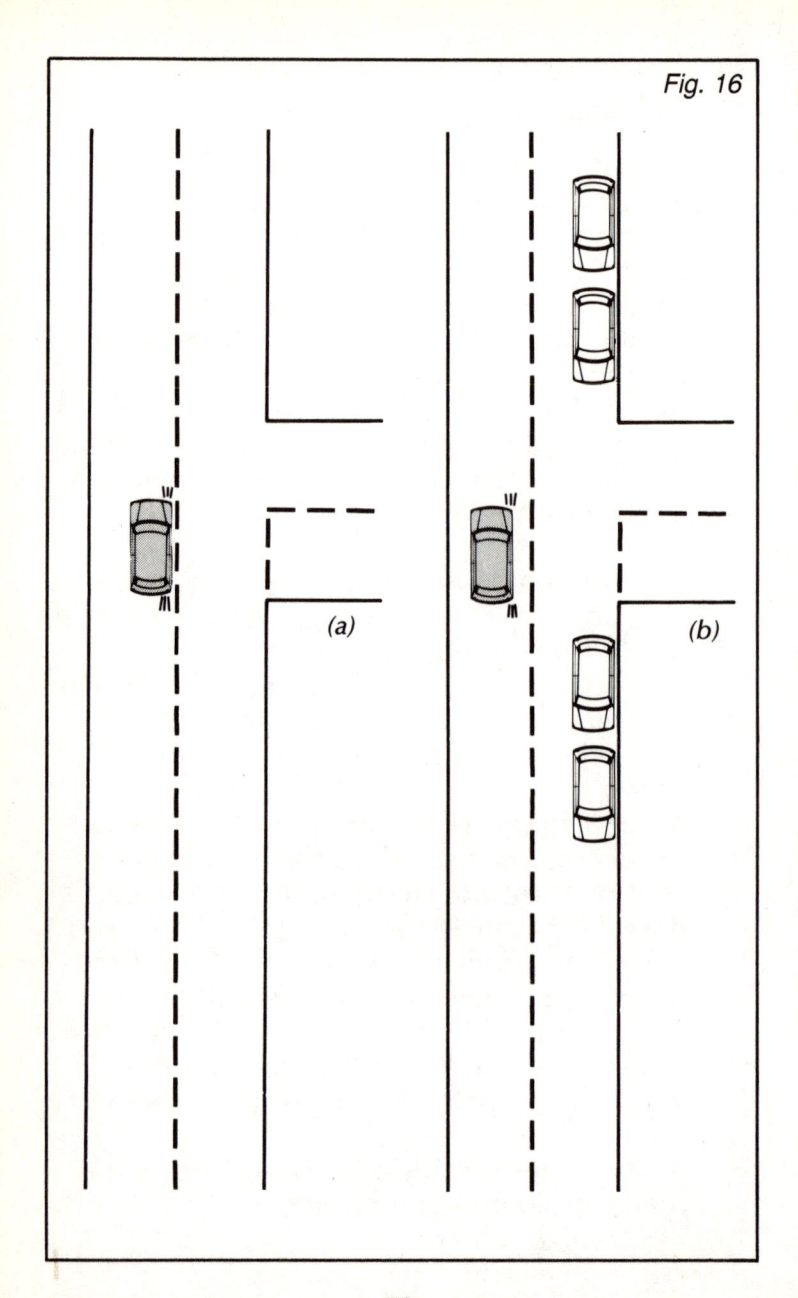

21 The reverse

Test requirements: 6, 8

This is the part of the test that most candidates fear. The most usual reason for failure on the 'reverse' is simply not enough practice beforehand. If you enter for the test feeling uncertain about any part of it, you are going to rely on luck and cannot expect to pass. The 'reverse' does require lots of practice and, though it is not an easy manoeuvre, it is, extremely important. You cannot expect the examiner to pass you if you cannot drive competently in *all* gears. (See Fig. 17.)

(1) The examiner will ask you to pull into the left before the road and explain what s/he wants you to do. As you drive past the road, check the gradient and the angle of the corner.

(2) Drive into a position about three car lengths from the corner, keeping about 45 centimetres (18 ins.) from the kerb. Check all round for traffic and then reverse slowly back.

(3) When you reach the corner, stop, check all round for traffic and, if clear, turn the wheel smoothly to the left while keeping the car moving slowly.

(4) When you get to a position parallel to the kerb, turn the wheel smoothly back to straighten the vehicle.

(5) Reverse back until the examiner tells you to stop.

Fig. 17

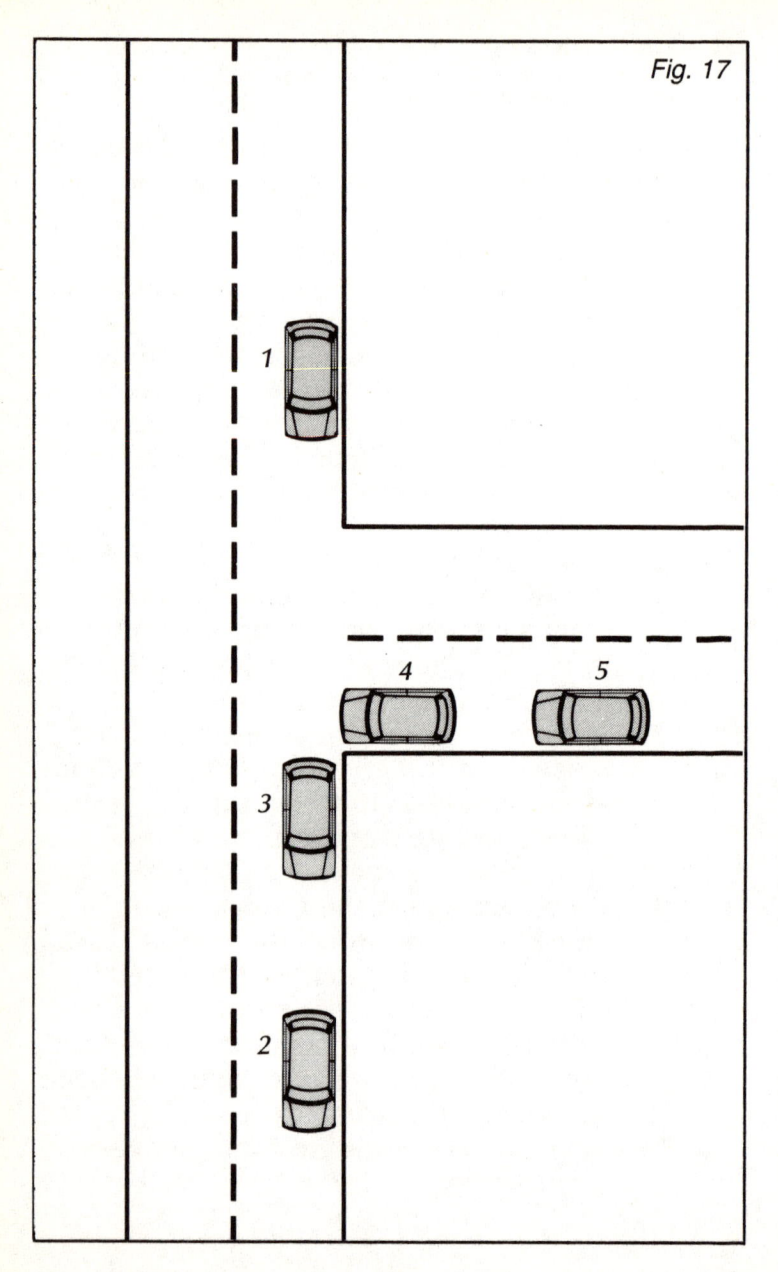

80

If you think of the reverse as a sequence of actions, as above, and take each one in turn, it should pass off smoothly.

Should it go slightly wrong and you swing wide or drive into the kerb, you do not automatically fail. If you swing wide, move slowly back into the kerb; do not rush yourself as you may then hit it. If you turn too tightly and feel that you are going to hit the kerb, stop immediately, use first gear and drive forward to straighten up, then reverse back again when safe. There is no need to start the whole manoeuvre again.

Observation on the 'reverse' is of paramount importance. All other road users have precedence over you, so if any are around you must wait for them to pass. If a vehicle drives down the road you are reversing into, you will need to drive around the corner and start again. Unless you are driving a very old car, when you put the gear lever into reverse, white instead of red lights shine at the back of the car to warn other road users. However, do not assume everybody knows this and, if necessary, move out of the way.

Obviously, not all corners are the same. If the corner you meet is as in Fig. 18 (a), a full lock on the wheel will be needed to ensure you do not swing wide. If the corner is the same as Fig. 18 (b), you will need to follow the kerb by turning the wheel slowly.

You may take your seat-belt off for the reverse but do not forget to put it back on before driving away.

The major point with the 'reverse' is *practice*.

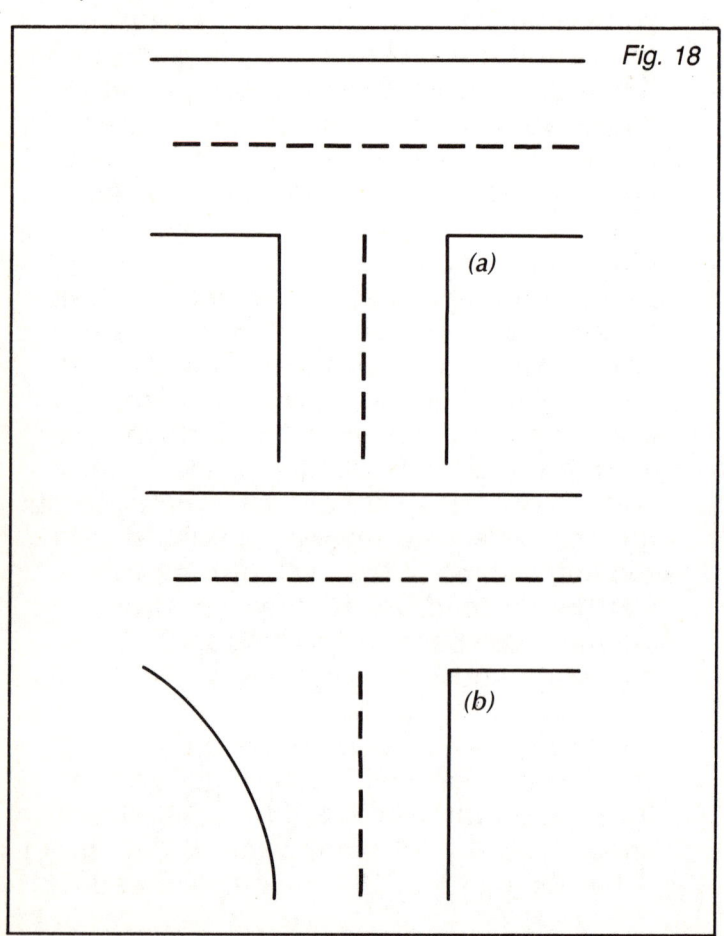

Fig. 18

22 Unmarked Crossroads

Test requirements: 3, 9, 12, 14, 20

You will find that road markings are not painted at the ends of every road. It would be prohibitively expensive to do this. Where there are no markings, it is usually because the right of way is obvious. However, there are occasions where the right of way is not obvious, but still there are no markings. This may be because the road has recently been resurfaced or simply the paint has worn out and not been replaced.

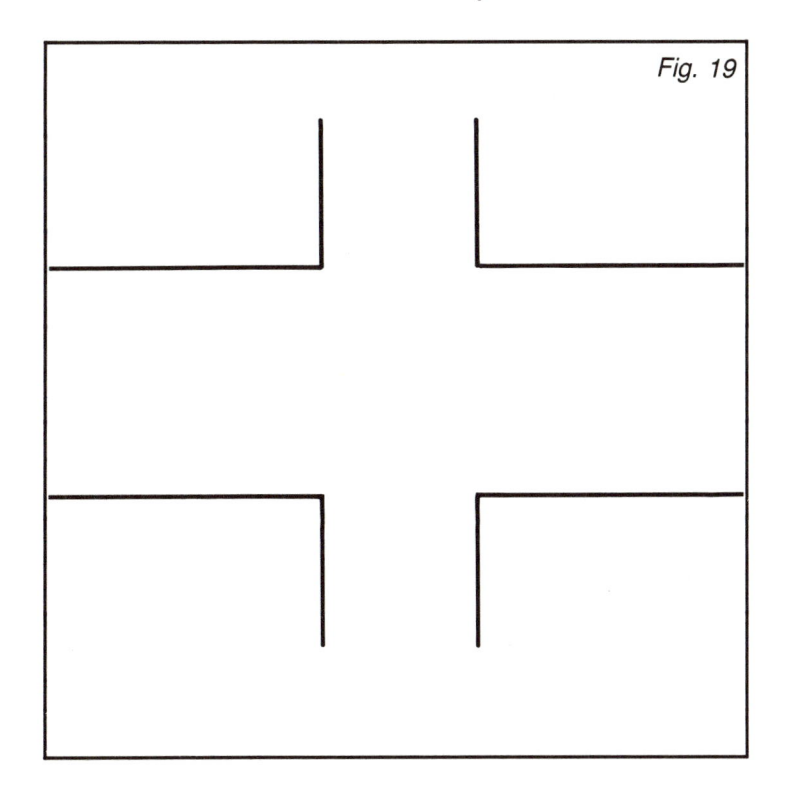

Fig. 19

In Fig. 19, you would assume that the larger road is the main road and you would have priority driving along it. This is not necessarily true. If there are no markings or signs to indicate otherwise, both roads at an unmarked crossroads have equal priority.

As you approach any crossroads, even those with road markings, you must check both side roads, as you cannot assume all other drivers will behave as they should. If you are in any doubt as to who has priority, assume you do not and be prepared to give way.

23 One-way streets

Test requirements: 9, 10, 11, 14, 16, 20

It is very likely you will meet either a one-way street or a one-way system on your test. The examiner will not inform you it is a one-way street but will expect you to notice.

Fig. 20 (a) shows the correct way to enter a one-way street. You will not fail if you enter the road as in Fig. 20 (b), but it is not correct.

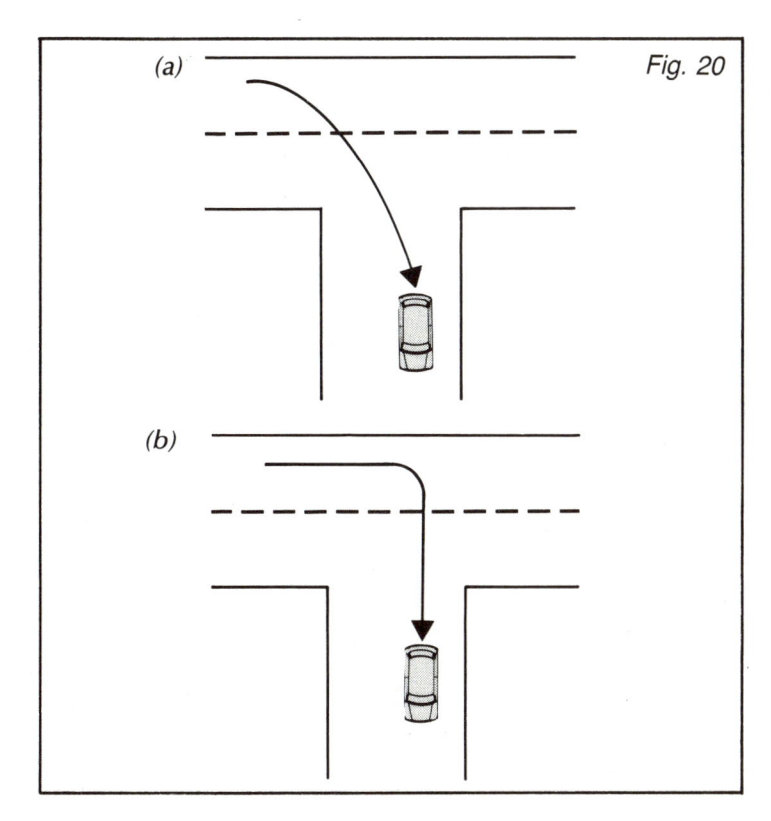

Fig. 20

If, as in our test route, you need to turn right at the end of the road, you must move to the right-hand side of the road as early as possible. Your exit position should be as in Fig. 21.

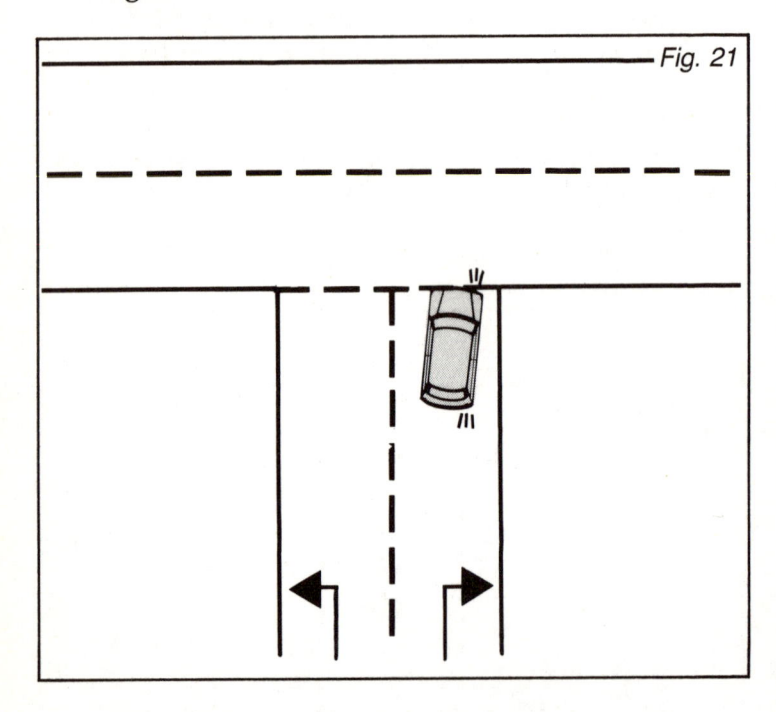

Fig. 21

One-way systems have become increasingly popular in towns and cities as they cut down traffic congestion by making everybody drive in the same direction. There are always plenty of signs to inform you which lane to take and you will need to pay attention to these as the examiner may ask you to follow a certain sign.

Fig. 22

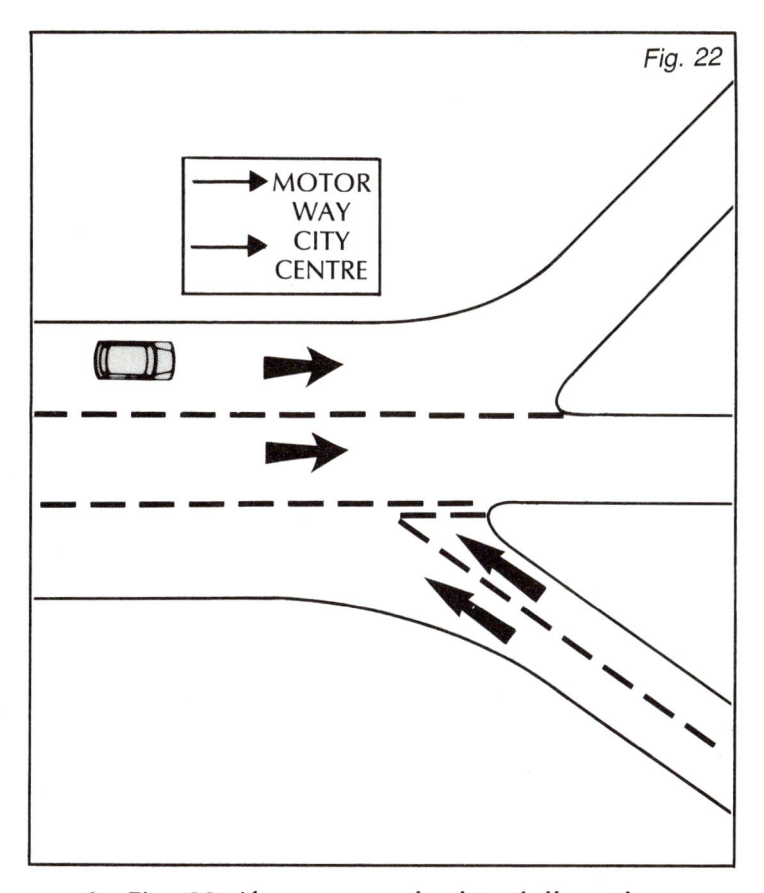

In Fig. 22, if you are asked to follow the signs to the city centre, you will need to move into the right-hand lane and stay in that lane until you see another sign or the examiner gives you further directions.

It pays to familiarise yourself with any awkward one-way systems in the vicinity of the test centre prior to your actual test.

24 Downhill start

Test requirements: 3, 4, 9, 10, 19, 20

You will not necessarily do a particular exercise to show the examiner a downhill start but there will doubtless be occasions where you need to move away when facing downhill.

It is imperative that you retain full control over the car at all times. Therefore, the procedure should be as follows:

(1) Select gear, usually first, but if the road is steep enough use second gear to start.
(2) Hold the car with the footbrake and release the handbrake.
(3) Check the mirrors and indicate if clear.
(4) Look over your shoulder.
(5) Take your foot off the brake and move it over to the accelerator as you let the clutch up. Steer out into the road.

If you start in this way, the car will not rush off down the hill and you will have both hands on the wheel to do any steering that is necessary.

25 Straight across a junction

Test requirements: 3, 9, 11, 14, 15, 20

At the beginning of the test the examiner has asked you to follow the road unless told to turn. Should you approach a junction at which s/he wishes you to continue straight ahead, s/he will say nothing. This is to make sure you notice the junction.

As you approach, treat it the same as any junction and slow down in plenty of time. Keep looking right, left and right as you cross. (See Fig. 23.) If there is a STOP sign you will, of course, be expected to stop.

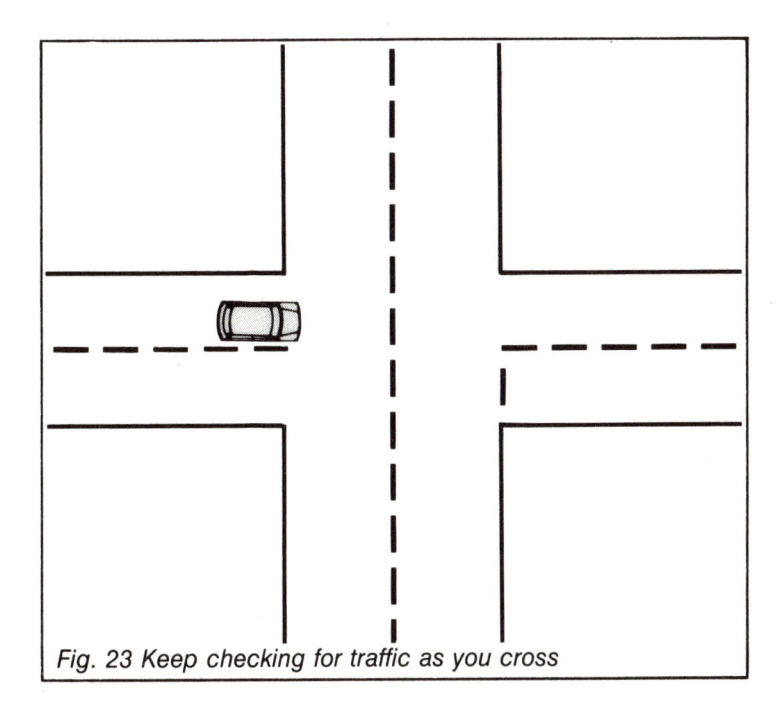

Fig. 23 Keep checking for traffic as you cross

26 Straight ahead at a roundabout

Test requirements: 3, 9, 10, 11, 13, 14, 15, 20

See Fig. 24. As you approach the roundabout, stay to the left. Keep to the left as you drive round the roundabout. As with the right turn, you should continue in second gear if the way is clear.

You must indicate left at **X** to inform other road users you intend to leave the roundabout.

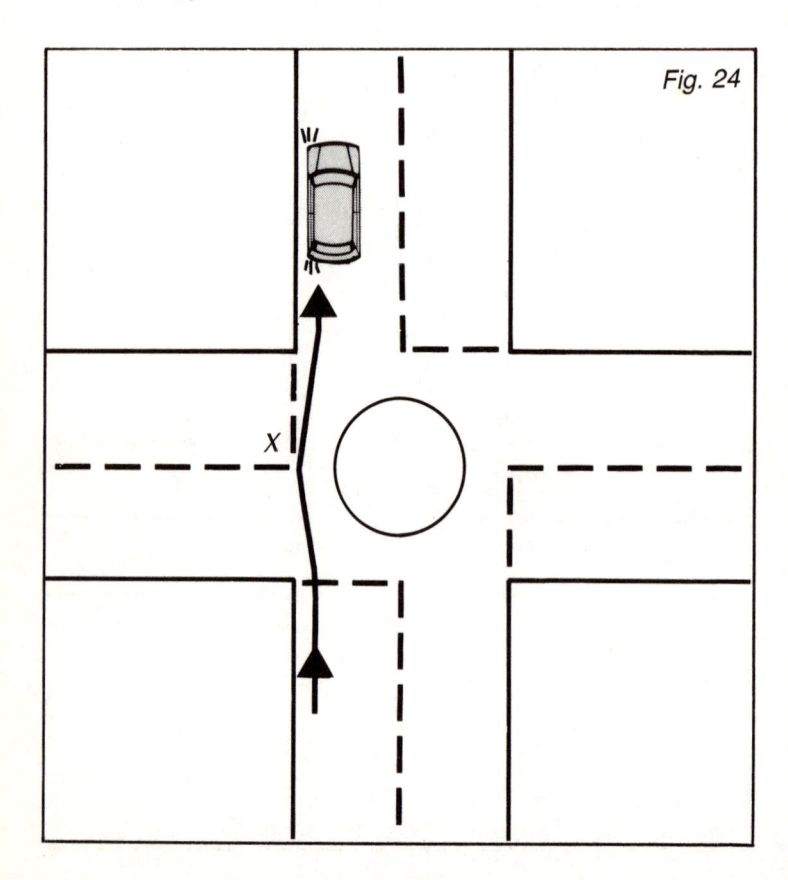

Fig. 24

27 Pelican crossing

Test requirements: 9, 11, 12, 18, 20

The rules of a Pelican crossing are:
(1) Red — stop.
(2) Amber — stop.
(3) Amber flashing — give way to pedestrians.
(4) Green — proceed if clear.

When the amber light is flashing, do not rev your engine to hurry pedestrians along. Wait until they have completely crossed and check for any that hurry onto the road trying to beat the lights.

28 Right turn onto a dual-carriageway

Test requirements: 3, 9, 10, 11, 14, 15, 20

Traffic will be travelling faster on a dual carriageway. Therefore you will need to look further along the road to be certain it is safe to enter.

There are two ways of joining a dual carriageway. How you tackle it will depend on the way the central reservation is laid out.

In Fig. 25 (a), there is not enough room for a car to wait in the middle and so the road must be clear both ways before you enter.

In Fig. 25 (b), there is enough space to wait in the middle and here you should treat the dual carriageway as two separate roads. Cross the first side and wait in the centre for the opposite side to be clear.

In both cases, as you join the dual carriageway you should drive into the left-hand lane, leaving the right-hand lane clear for traffic to overtake.

Once on the dual carriageway, if the signs and conditions dictate, you may be able to drive faster than 30 m.p.h.

Fig. 25

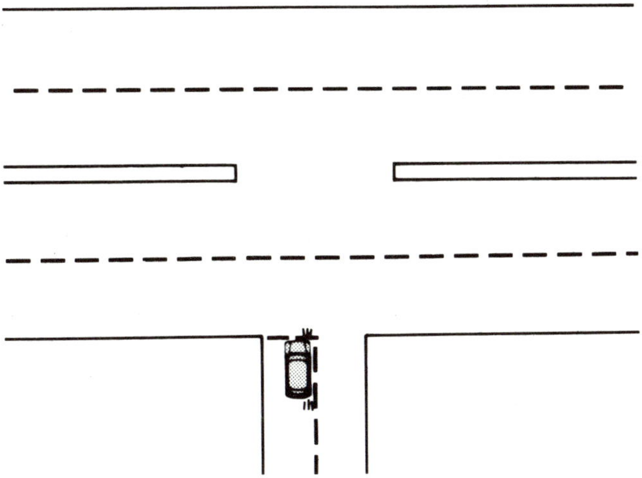

(a)

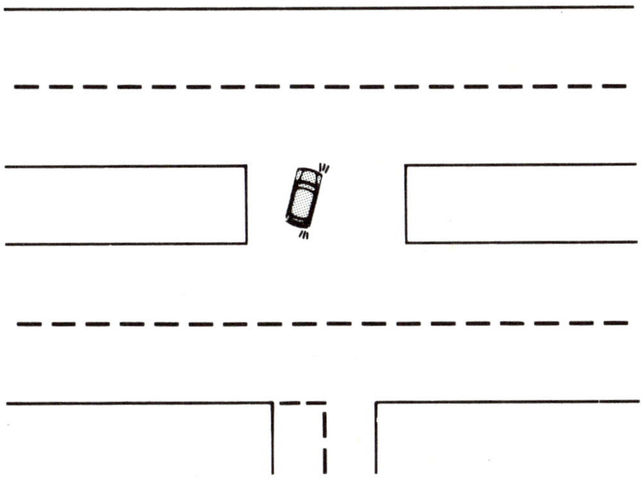

(b)

29 Turning right off a dual carriageway

Test requirements: 3, 9, 10, 11, 12, 13, 14, 15, 16, 20

See Fig. 26. When you are asked to turn right, act promptly as the traffic will be moving fast. Check the mirror and signal. If a car is overtaking, wait until it has passed, check your side mirror and blind spot and move smoothly into the right-hand lane. Drive into the gap in the central reservation, following any road markings there may be.

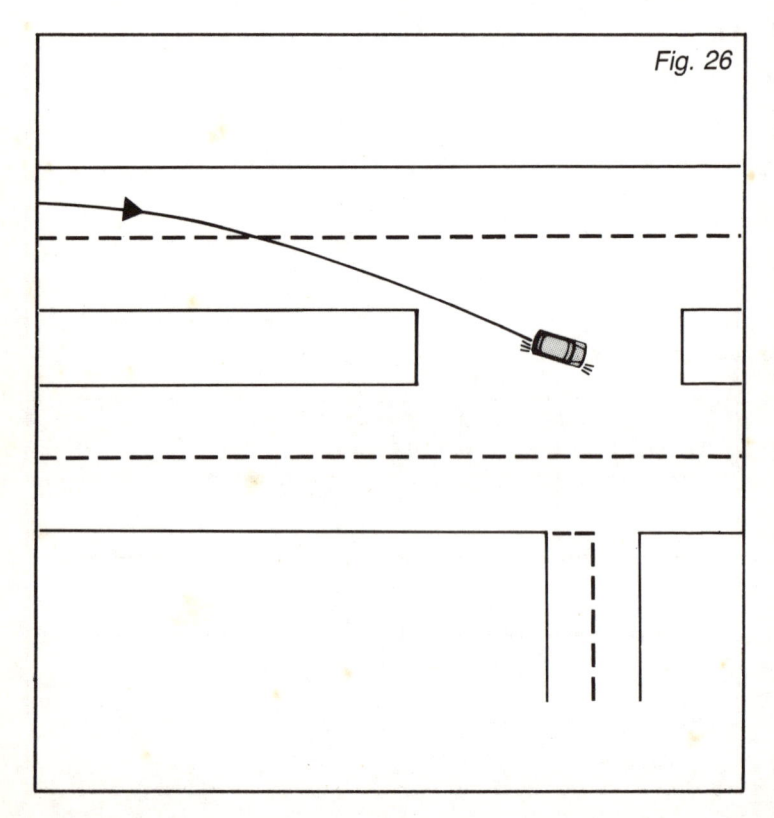

Fig. 26

When the opposite carriageway is clear, steer smoothly across into the side road. The examiner will want to see the whole manoeuvre accomplished calmly, so ensure you take it at a speed that will enable you to cope without hindering other road users.

Dual carriageways will not necessarily be included in your test, but you must feel confident in your ability to deal with them anyway. Many drivers tend to speed up rapidly as they enter a dual carriageway and have more accidents on them than anywhere else. So, always take great care when entering or leaving these roads.

30 A school

Test requirements: 9, 11, 12, 18, 20

Taking a test in an urban area generally involves passing a school somewhere. If children should be in classes at the time, do not assume that all of them are there. At the beginning and end of the school day, a crossing patrol could be in operation. Always obey the traffic controller and keep a lookout for any children crossing the road nearby or running into the road.

Most pedestrian fatalities happen to older people and children. Their actions can be very unpredictable so extra care must be taken when you see them.

At the end of your test you will be asked to pull in to the left and park reasonably close to the test centre. When you have parked, make sure the car is safe, i.e. handbrake on and gear lever in neutral, before switching the engine off. Take your seat-belt off and relax.

Here the examiner will inform you of your test result.

The driving test is quite concentrated as the examiners have only approximately 30 minutes to make a decision and must be sure you can fulfil all the requirements in that time. When you have passed you are unlikely to encounter all the hazards of a test in any one day but at some time or another you will meet them all.

Provided you have practised enough before the test, you should not find it too difficult. If you concentrate, look well ahead and give yourself time to react, everything should go smoothly. Examiners take no pleasure in failing you, but if you are not competent it would be unsafe for them to allow you on the road.

By the time you take the test, you should have satisfied yourself that you can cope safely with all the situations above. If you cannot truthfully answer 'yes', then you will need some luck to pass on the day. Luck has a tendency to desert us when we need it most and passing by luck has nothing to do with competence.

6
THE THEORY TEST

In the following pages you will find examples of the types of questions you will be required to answer when you sit the compulsory theory test which, as noted before, must be passed before you can take the practical driving test. Answers are given on page 128 and will also be found in the Highway Code, but we suggest you go through and mark your answers with a pencil before checking. This should help to determine where the gaps in your knowledge lie and enable you to revise these areas in detail.

The questions in the theory test itself fall into four categories, namely:

Alertness and attitude
These refer to the need for total concentration, the ability to be aware of and anticipate the actions of other road users and to drive with consideration and courtesy towards others.

The safety of your vehicle, safety margins, vehicle handling and vehicle loading
These questions are designed to make sure you know what to do to keep your vehicle in good order and how to drive it safely in all conditions.

Hazard awareness, vulnerable road users, other types of vehicle
These questions will test your ability to recognise hazards and plan ahead, to be aware of vulnerable road users such as children and cyclists and to recognise that large vehicles require more space on the roads. Your knowledge of the effects of alcohol, drugs and tiredness on driving ability will also be tested.

Motorway rules, rules of the road, road and traffic signs, documents, accidents
These topics are self-explanatory!

The test takes the form of 35 multiple choice questions, which need to be answered in 40 minutes. In most cases you need to identify one correct answer from a choice of four, although some will require two or more correct answers from a selection. It is wise to attempt to answer all the questions, even if you are not completely sure of the answer in some cases. To pass, you will need at least 30 correct answers.

Remember, the test questions will not necessarily include any of the following examples, which are given as a guide only to help you be aware of the areas of your knowledge which perhaps require special attention.

QUESTIONS ON EVERYDAY SITUATIONS

1 *Which two of the following are legal requirements for the condition of your tyres?*
(a) Minimum tread depth of 1 mm
(b) Tread visible over the whole tyre
(c) Minimum tread depth of 1.6 mm
(d) All tyres to be of the same make

2 *At what age is a car required to have an M.O.T. Certificate?*
(a) 1 year
(b) 2 years
(c) 3 years
(d) 4 years

3 *What would the speed limit be in a built-up area?*
(a) 30 mph.
(b) 30 mph. unless road signs show otherwise
(c) 40 mph.
(d) 40 mph. unless road signs show otherwise

4 *What colour follows red at traffic lights?*
(a) Amber
(b) Flashing amber
(c) Red and amber
(d) Green

5 *At a pelican crossing what colour follows red?*
(a) Amber
(b) Red and amber
(c) Flashing amber
(d) Green

6 *At a pelican crossing you see a flashing amber light. Should you:*
(a) stop?
(b) proceed?
(c) proceed providing the crossing is clear of pedestrians?
(d) wait for a green light?

7 *What is the overall stopping distance of a car travelling at 40 mph. on a dry road?*
(a) 36 metres
(b) 23 metres
(c) 53 metres
(d) 60 metres

8 *On wet roads will the stopping distance be:*
(a) the same?
(b) doubled?
(c) ten times?
(d) five times?

9 *When must you not sound your horn?*
(a) Between the hours of 11.00 pm and 6.00 am
(b) Between the hours of 11.30 pm and 7.00 am in a built-up area
(c) Midnight to 6.00 am
(d) Between 10 pm and 6 am

10 *Another driver flashes his headlights. Should you:*
   (a) assume he is giving way to you?
   (b) proceed?
   (c) proceed if you are sure it is safe to do so?
   (d) flash your headlights back?

11 *Which two of the following must you not do within the zig-zag lines on approach to a pedestrian crossing?*
   (a) Stop
   (b) Park
   (c) Sound your horn
   (d) Overtake

12 *You **must not** overtake in which two of the following situations?*
   (a) In a 30 mph. speed limit
   (b) Within the zig-zag area at a pedestrian crossing
   (c) On a straight road
   (d) If you would have to straddle double white lines where the solid line is nearest you

13 *What is the last thing to do before moving away from the side of the road?*
   (a) Indicate
   (b) Put on your seatbelt
   (c) Look over your shoulder into the blind spot
   (d) Check your mirror

14 *How would you inform a pedestrian at a zebra crossing that you intend to stop and allow him to cross?*
   (a) Wave him across the road
   (b) Use a slowing down hand signal
   (c) Sound your horn
   (d) Nod your head and smile

15 *If you cannot see clearly behind you when reversing what should you do?*
   (a) Use the mirrors
   (b) Ask someone to assist you
   (c) Carry on regardless
   (d) Stop the car and check

16 *If someone is reversing into your path, what would be your first action?*
   (a) Speed up to get past them
   (b) Sound your horn as a warning
   (c) Ignore them
   (d) Reverse

17 *What lights should you switch on at dusk?*
   (a) Fog lights
   (b) Side lights
   (c) Dipped headlights
   (d) Headlights

18 *When parking on the street at night where should you park?*
   (a) Anywhere
   (b) On the left hand side of the road
   (c) Only in parking bays
   (d) Under a street lamp

19 *Where may you overtake another vehicle on the left?*
 (a) On a motorway
 (b) In a one-way street
 (c) Where there is not enough space on the right
 (d) It is never permissible to overtake on the left

QUESTIONS ON UNUSUAL SITUATIONS

1 *How would you know if a pedestrian was blind and deaf?*
 (a) S/he would have a hearing aid
 (b) S/he would have a white stick
 (c) His/her white stick would have two red reflective bands
 (d) S/he would have a guide dog

2 *What should you do when driving past animals?*
 (a) Sound your horn
 (b) Get past as quickly as possible
 (c) Rev the engine to hurry them up
 (d) Drive past slowly and stop if necessary

3 *What should you do if an emergency vehicle approaches from behind with its siren on?*
 (a) Ignore it and carry on
 (b) Move over to the left as soon as it is safe to do so
 (c) Speed up to keep in front of it
 (d) Stop

4 *What is the speed limit on a dual carriageway?*
   (a) 50 mph.
   (b) 60 mph.
   (c) 70 mph.
   (d) 70 mph. unless road signs show otherwise

5 *When driving in fog what are the two most important things to consider?*
   (a) Keeping close to the rear lights of the car in front
   (b) Using dipped headlights
   (c) Maintaining a high speed
   (d) Using windscreen wipers

6 *The main cause of skidding is:*
   (a) The driver
   (b) The vehicle
   (c) The road conditions
   (d) The weather conditions

7 *Having just driven through flood water, what should you check on your car?*
   (a) The engine
   (b) The steering
   (c) The brakes
   (d) The lights

8 *What should you do if you are involved in a minor accident?*
   (a) Drive on
   (b) Stop
   (c) Phone the emergency services
   (d) Phone a garage

9 *If you breakdown on a motorway and have a red warning triangle, how far behind your car should you place it?*
 (a)   5 metres
 (b) 50 metres
 (c) 150 metres
 (d) 200 metres

10 *What is the first thing to do if you break down on a level crossing?*
 (a) Push the car clear of the crossing
 (b) Phone the signalman
 (c) Get you and your passengers clear of the crossing
 (d) Phone the emergency services

11 *If, when driving at night, an oncoming vehicle approaches with headlights on full beam, should you:*
 (a) flash your headlights?
 (b) speed up to get past quicker?
 (c) slow down and avert your eyes, stopping if necessary?
 (d) put your headlights on full beam too?

QUESTIONS ON MOTORWAY DRIVING

1 *You may stop on the hard shoulder of a motorway:*
  (a) to exercise your dog?
  (b) to have a rest?
  (c) to make a phone call?
  (d) in an emergency?

2 *The right hand lane on a motorway should be used:*
  (a) for fast drivers only?
  (b) for overtaking?
  (c) all the time?
  (d) only if you are in a hurry?

3 *What is the speed limit on a motorway?*
  (a) 60 mph.
  (b) 70 mph. unless otherwise stated
  (c) 30 mph.
  (d) 50 mph.

4 *You would find red reflectors (catseyes) where on the motorway?*
  (a) Separating the lanes
  (b) The left hand side
  (c) The right hand side
  (d) The left and right hand side

5 *If you see red lights flashing over your lane, what must you do?*
(a) Be prepared to slow down
(b) Leave the motorway
(c) Proceed no further in that lane
(d) Slow down immediately

6 *Which three of the following must you not do on a motorway?*
(a) Reverse
(b) Keep to the speed limit
(c) Drive in the left hand lane
(d) Cross the central reservation
(e) Hitch-hike
(f) Overtake

7 *What should you do if something falls off your vehicle on a motorway?*
(a) Stop and retrieve it
(b) Stop at the first emergency phone and inform the police
(c) Carry on and phone the police later
(d) Phone the emergency services

TRAFFIC SIGNS

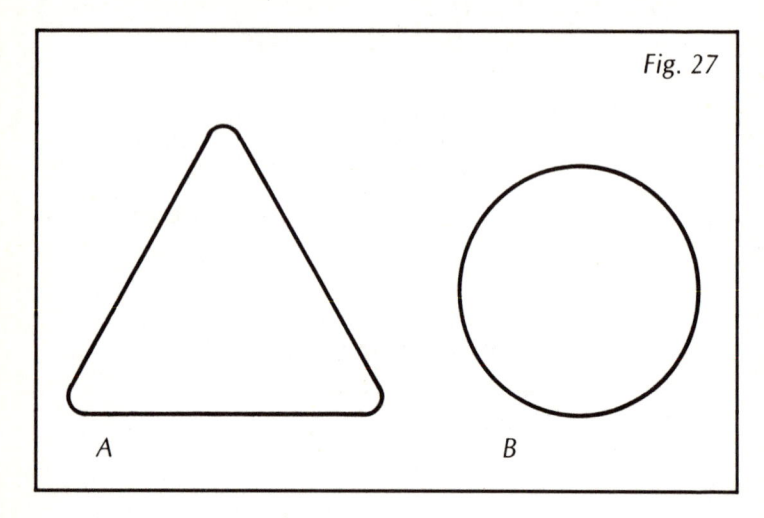

Fig. 27

A   B

1 *Does the triangular sign (A) in Fig. 27 generally give:*
   (a) a warning?
   (b) information?
   (c) direction?
   (d) speed limit?

2 *Does the circular sign (B) in Fig. 27 generally give:*
   (a) an order?
   (b) a warning?
   (c) the end of minimum speed limits?
   (d) information?

3 *What do the signs in Fig. 28 mean?*

Fig. 28

C

D

E

F

G

H

I

J

K

L

M

N

C means:
(a) no overtaking
(b) overtaking allowed
(c) beware of parked cars
(d) keep left

D means:
(a) give priority to vehicles from the opposite direction
(b) heavy traffic in opposite lane
(c) end of dual carriageway
(d) diversion ahead

E means:
(a) no speed limit
(b) national speed limit applies
(c) increase speed
(d) end of restriction

F means:
(a) turn left
(b) turn left ahead
(c) bend ahead
(d) pull into the side of the road

G means:
(a) keep left
(b) turn left
(c) beware of traffic from the left
(d) no left turn

H means:
(a) beware of traffic on the inside lane
(b) turn left
(c) keep left
(d) move into inside lane

I means:
(a) road narrows
(b) road narrows on both sides
(c) entering a built-up area
(d) slow down

J means:
(a) no overtaking ahead
(b) road narrows
(c) dual carriageway ends
(d) limited room to overtake

K means:
(a) change to opposite carriageway
(b) cross central reservation
(c) bend in the road
(d) one way traffic ahead

L means:
(a) steep hill going down
(b) steep hill upwards
(c) light vehicles only
(d) restriction ahead

M means:
(a) traffic merges from left
(b) traffic merges from left with equal priority
(c) traffic merges from right with equal priority
(d) major junction ahead

N means:
(a) traffic merges from left
(b) traffic merges from left with equal priority
(c) traffic merges from right
(d) traffic merges from right with equal priority

ROAD MARKINGS

1 *What do the road markings in Fig. 29 mean?*

A means:
(a) warning of 'give way' just ahead
(b) road widens ahead
(c) you have priority ahead
(d) stop ahead

B means:
(a) box junction
(b) approaching traffic lights
(c) approaching zebra crossing
(d) no parking

Fig. 29

A

B Yellow markings

C D E F

C means:
(a) line indicating hard shoulder
(b) centre line
(c) lane line
(d) give way

D means:
(a) centre line
(b) you are on a dual carriageway
(c) no overtaking
(d) you may overtake

E means:
(a) no overtaking
(b) parking allowed
(c) keep left
(d) hazard warning line

F means:
(a) you must not enter this area
(b) chevrons, to separate streams of traffic
(c) limited visibility ahead
(d) concealed entrance

2   *What do the road markings in Fig. 30 mean?*

G means:
(a) stop line
(b) give way to traffic on major roads
(c) hazard warning line
(d) lane line

Fig. 30

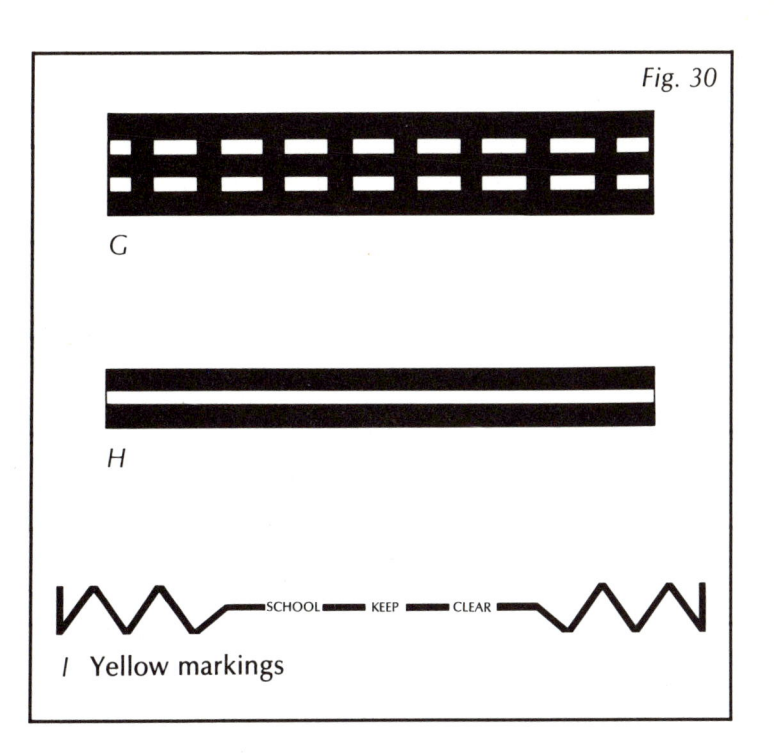

G

H

/ Yellow markings

H means:
(a) centre line
(b) stop line at STOP sign
(c) lane line
(d) give way line

I means:
(a) keep entrance clear even when picking up or setting down children
(b) keep crossing clear
(c) keep clear except when picking up or setting down children
(d) keep clear during school hours

MOTORWAY SIGNS

There are four motorway signs illustrated in Fig. 31.

A means:
(a) keep left
(b) change lane
(c) leave the motorway at the next exit
(d) reduce your speed

B means:
(a) left hand bend ahead
(b) take the next exit off the motorway
(c) change lane
(d) hazard in left hand lane

C means:
(a) lane closed ahead
(b) fast traffic in left hand lanes
(c) no overtaking
(d) slow down

D means:
(a) end of diversion
(b) end of restriction
(c) end of motorway ahead
(d) end of speed limit

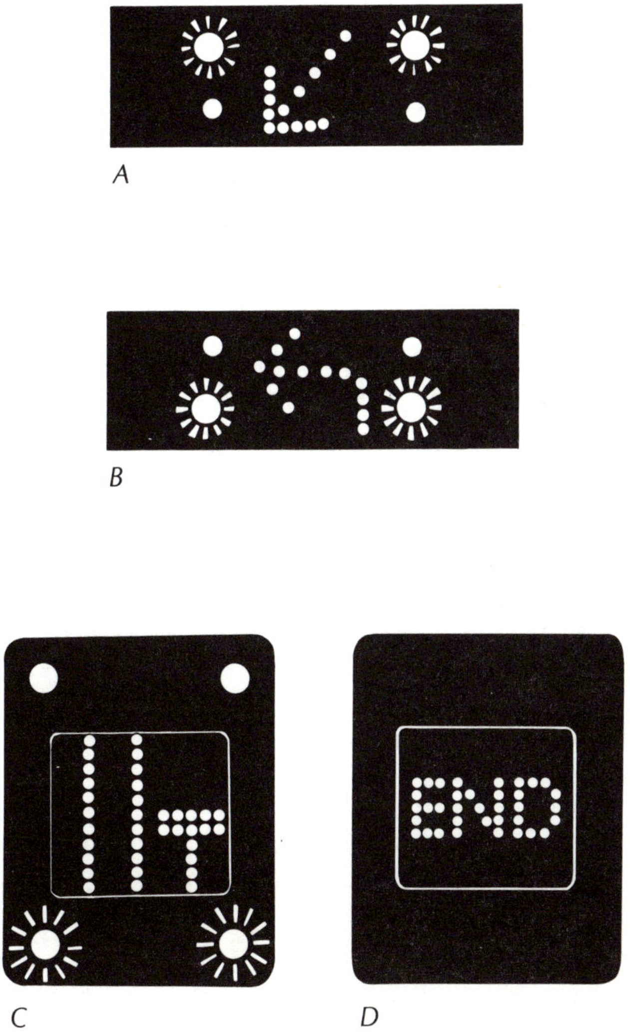

Fig. 31

A

B

C *D*

7
THE RESULTS

Q *What happens when I pass?*
A You will normally be notified of the theory test result within 10 working days of taking the test and if successful will receive a pass certificate. To pass you must gain 30 marks out of a possible 35, but you will not be told your pass mark. If you pass the practical test, the examiner will tell you at the end of the test and will give you a pass certificate which you must send to the D.V.L.C at Swansea together with your provisional licence. No fee is payable for this.

Q *Can I drive straight away?*
A Yes, take a note of your 'driver number' and keep it with you while your licence is away.

Q *Can I drive an automatic if I pass in a manual car?*
A Yes.

Q *Should I take more lessons?*
A All driving experience gained with a qualified instructor will stand you in good stead. It helps to drive on a motorway for the first time with an instructor.

Q *Should I take an advanced test?*
A Yes. If everybody took an advanced test, driving standards would undoubtedly improve. It is in your own best interest to take a pride in your driving.

Q *What should I do if I fail?*
A Apply immediately for another test. Do not be despondent, but think carefully about where you went wrong and work at it so that you are ready for the next test.

Q *Will the examiner discuss the points on which I failed?*
A S/he will tell you what you did wrong in order to help you but an examiner is not permitted to discuss intricate details relating to the test. If you fail the theory test you are not told your marks or what you failed on.

Q *Can I appeal against the examiner's decision?*
A The only grounds for appeal is if the test was not conducted properly. You cannot appeal against the result.

8
CONCLUSION

In this book, we have covered everything you need to know to pass a driving test, but do remember there is more to driving than simply passing the test.

There are numerous situations you will not have encountered before taking the test, and these will need to be dealt with competently and safely. Driving is a skill that you never stop learning.

Being able to drive gives you a new-found freedom but also great responsibility. Whenever you get into the driving seat of a car you must realise your responsibility to yourself, your passengers and all other road users. In the wrong hands, a car can be a very dangerous weapon. Always take a pride in your driving.

Good luck.

9
NOTES FOR AFTER THE TEST

While learning to drive, you have probably used someone else's car — a driving school car or possibly your parents' or a friend's car. Now that you have passed, it is time to get one of your own and become truly independent. The following questions will, hopefully, set you off on the right foot.

Q *How much should I pay for a car?*
A Cars are expensive. After a house, a car is the second largest purchase you are likely to make in your life. Do not rush to buy the first one you see; there are very few real bargains around, and you tend to get what you pay for. Work out a realistic budget before you look, and remember all the other incidentals.

Q *What are these 'other incidentals'?*
A A car must be taxed and insured. Car tax is currently £145 a year (1997) and as a new driver you may find the cost of insurance quite high. Also you must keep the car in a roadworthy condition and, unless you buy a new car, it is likely that some work will need to be done.

Q *Should I learn about car maintenance?*
A The more you know about your car the more time and money you will save yourself in the future.

Q *Should I have my car serviced by a garage?*
A Unless you feel confident in your mechanical ability, it would be better to seek the services of an expert. Having a car serviced regularly does prolong its life and probably pays for itself in the long run. If the car you buy is three years old or more you must get an M.O.T. certificate once a year.

Q *How should I prepare my car for winter?*
A Check there is enough anti-freeze in the cooling system, that the tyres are not too worn, the windscreen wiper blades are functioning effectively and the lights and brakes are in full working order.

Q *What extra precautions should I take in snow?*
A If possible, keep the car in a garage when you are not using it. If you are advised by the police to drive only if your journey is vital, then use your car only if you must. If you cannot avoid driving, allow a lot longer for the journey, keep a good distance from the vehicle in front and use the brakes very gently.

Q *What about driving at night?*
A Driving at night is very different from driving in daytime. You may not be able to see familiar landmarks and will have to follow the road signs more closely. There is, obviously, less traffic on the roads and if you are undertaking a long journey, it can be easier to do so during the night. However, you may feel sleepy so take plenty of breaks and get out of the car to stretch your legs. Pedestrians are very difficult to see at night, so keep an extra-special lookout.

Q *What if it is raining at night?*
A You will experience a lot of glare from other lights in the rain. Do not let your eyes get drawn to the lights, concentrate on the road in front of you and keep your speed down.

Q *What is different about driving on a motorway?*
A The speed you will be travelling at is a lot higher than you have been used to up till now. Always drive within your own capabilities and allow yourself enough time to get used to the speed of the other traffic before you drive fast yourself. Although there is a speed limit of 70 mph. on motorways, a lot of cars are capable of 120 mph. and more, and the fact is, there will be a lot of people driving faster than 70 mph. What is needed is frequent checks in the mirror and when overtaking allow yourself plenty of time to move out and back into lane.

The other point about motorway driving is that it can be very boring and your mind may tend to wander or you may feel sleepy. There are service stations at regular intervals, so do not push yourself — pull in and take a break. When leaving a motorway, be careful to adjust your speed.

Q *What essentials should I carry in the car?*
A 1 Driving licence.
2 Insurance details.
3 Spare petrol can (empty).
4 Cloth for the windows.
5 Spare bulbs for the back lights.
In addition, during the winter, also have:
1 A shovel.
2 De-icer.

3 A windscreen scraper.
4 An old coat or blanket.

Q *Must I always carry my licence with me?*
A No, but it is advisable. If you are stopped by the police and you do not have your licence with you it must be produced at a police station within five days.

Q *What should I do if I am stopped by the police?*
A The police will stop you only if they think you are committing an offence. Always be courteous; most traffic violations are minor offences and if you are polite you may be given only a verbal warning.

Q *What are the rules concerning drink/driving?*
A You must not drive with a blood alcohol level higher than 80 mg/100 ml. Different people react in different ways to drink and it is better not to drink at all if you are driving. Drink/driving is a very serious offence and the very least you will get away with is a large fine and the loss of your licence.

Answers to Questions in Chapter 6

Questions on Everyday Situations (page 101)

1 (b), (c)
2 (c)
3 (b)
4 (c)
5 (c)
6 (c)
7 (a)
8 (b)
9 (b)
10 (c)
11 (b), (d)
12 (b), (d)
13 (c)
14 (b)
15 (b)
16 (b)
17 (c)
18 (b)
19 (b)

Questions on Unusual Situations (page 105)

1 (c)
2 (d)
3 (b)
4 (d)
5 (b), (d)
6 (a)
7 (c)
8 (b)
9 (c)
10 (c)
11 (c)

Questions on Motorway Driving (page 108)

1 (d)
2 (b)
3 (b)
4 (b)
5 (c)
6 (a), (d), (e)
7 (b)

Traffic Signs (page 110)

1 (a)
2 (a)
3 C (a)
  D (a)
  E (b)
  F (b)
  G (b)
  H (c)
3 I (b)
  J (c)
  K (a)
  L (b)
  M (b)
  N (d)

Road Markings (page 114)

1 A (a)
  B (a)
  C (c)
  D (a)
  E (d)
  F (b)
2 G (b)
  H (b)
  I (a)

Motorway Signs (page 118)

A (b)
B (b)
C (a)
D (b)

128